Understanding Russian Black Sea Power Dynamics Through National Security Gaming

ANIKA BINNENDIJK

RAND NATIONAL DEFENSE RESEARCH INSTITUTE

Prepared for the Office of the Secretary of Defense
Approved for public release

For more information on this publication, visit www.rand.org/t/RR3094

Library of Congress Cataloging-in-Publication Data is available for this publication.
ISBN: 978-1-9774-0345-2

Published by the RAND Corporation, Santa Monica, Calif.
© Copyright 2020 RAND Corporation
RAND® is a registered trademark.

Cover: LA(Phot) Guy Pool/Wikimedia Commons (submarine); kdow/iStock/ Getty Images Plus (background map of the Black Sea).

Support RAND
Make a tax-deductible charitable contribution at
www.rand.org/giving/contribute

www.rand.org

Preface

Recent Russian military investment in its Black Sea posture since 2014 has profoundly altered the security map of the region. While NATO has taken some steps to assert presence in the Black Sea, the United States and its regional allies may have a limited set of military options with which to further expand existing defense and deterrence measures. This project sought to identify dimensions of Russian power in the Black Sea region and assess their potential implications for Western military options during a regional crisis. The project developed a scenario-based game, drawing from research on Russian military, economic, and political activities across the Black Sea region. The game, held June 2018, explored regional allied and partner considerations in a decision to further enhance Western military defense and deterrence activities, as well as the multidimensional tactics that Russia might employ to thwart these measures. The research reported here was completed in June 2019 and underwent security review with the sponsor and the Defense Office of Prepublication and Security Review before public release.

This research was sponsored by the Office of the Secretary of Defense and conducted within the International Security and Defense Policy Center of the RAND National Security Research Division (NSRD), which operates the RAND National Defense Research Institute (NDRI), a federally funded research and development center (FFRDC) sponsored by the Office of the Secretary of Defense, the Joint Staff, the Unified Combatant Commands, the Navy, the Marine Corps, the defense agencies, and the defense intelligence enterprise.

For more information on the RAND International Security and Defense Policy Center, see http://www.rand.org/nsrd/ndri/centers/isdp or contact the Center director (contact information provided on the webpage).

Contents

Figures

Tables

Summary

This project sought to explore the dynamics associated with a potentially escalatory military crisis in the Black Sea, and particularly how Russia might apply multidimensional elements of power to influence and constrain regional decisionmaking concerning defense and deterrence options. RAND conducted a literature review to identify key areas of Russian military, political, and economic influence in the Black Sea region and applied the findings to create a card-based game in which players representing governments across the region, including Russia, were asked to respond to a notional scenario. The game was played by subject-matter experts at RAND's Washington, D.C., office in June 2018. The game and associated research (conducted January 2018–June 2019) yielded a number of insights of potential interest to policymakers and regional analysts. Specifically, these include the following:

- Russia has successfully altered the military status quo in the Black Sea to its advantage. Russia's control of Crimea, recent investment in the modernization of its Black Sea Fleet, deployments of air and coastal defense assets to the region, and deployment of additional ground troops to the Southern Military District have shifted the military balance in the Black Sea significantly.
- Black Sea allies and partners have a diverse range of interests and threat perceptions with respect to Russia, making it difficult to achieve consensus on a multilateral response to Russian military posturing in the absence of overt aggression.

- Russia would likely use a variety of gray-zone activities to undermine regional cohesion around a unified response before escalating to military measures. Russia's risk tolerance in the Black Sea would likely depend on its perceptions of potential losses; it would seek to achieve its objectives at minimal cost but would likely escalate if it felt that it were likely to experience significant losses in the region.
- Turkish support would be critical to any response, because of Turkish naval capabilities and responsibility for the straits under the Montreux Convention. Acute Turkish security interests in Syria and the need to maintain cooperation with Russia to address them, Turkey's deepening dependence on Russian natural gas imports with the completion of the TurkStream pipeline, and Turkish concerns about Russian military dominance could make Turkey reluctant to counter Russian aggression forcefully.
- Romania would likely have the will and the capability to contribute to a regional military initiative in the Black Sea. Ongoing military procurement, modernization, and expansion plans could enhance Romanian maritime contributions, and the Romanian government's interest in bolstering U.S. and North Atlantic Treaty Organization (NATO) presence in the Black Sea is likely to be deepened, rather than deterred, by Russian coercive pressures.
- Bulgaria remains vulnerable to Russian incentives and coercion. Russian integration in the Bulgarian energy sector may increase in the coming years as the second phase of the TurkStream project offers new a route for Russian gas to southeastern Europe via Bulgaria, and as the Russian state nuclear corporation Rosatom eyes financing of the previously halted Belene nuclear reactor project. Bulgarian wariness of Russian political meddling and military threats could once again prompt Bulgarian reluctance to support an initiative that would raise Moscow's ire.
- Georgian and Ukrainian military capabilities were significantly eroded in their respective conflicts with Russia, and their limited defense budgets are likely to constrain military modernization efforts for the foreseeable future. However, both countries

would be likely to seek a role in a regional initiative, including hosting rotational forces at Black Sea ports, and would welcome U.S. and other Western presences for expanded exercises and training programs.

Recommendations

RAND's 2018 Black Sea game suggested that a regional force imbalance such as the one Russia has recently established in the Black Sea not only undermines deterrence but may also reduce the willingness of some regional allies to support initiatives designed to manage a future crisis. That, in turn, could increase the risk of Russian miscalculation and unwanted escalation. Measures designed to strengthen regional allies and partners and reduce Russia's military advantage would serve to enhance both deterrence and the prospects of regional cooperation during a confrontation. The game simulated regional deliberations surrounding the establishment of a regional Black Sea task force. Short of this, interim measures might include further increases in the operations tempo of rotational U.S. and other NATO naval presences in the Black Sea, establishment of a NATO Black Sea Center of Excellence in Turkey, and expanded U.S. security cooperation programs and activities in the Black Sea, including additional excess defense article transfers. Additional analysis might explore the political feasibility of placement of NATO missile assets to defend Black Sea allied coasts, as well as the Bosporus Strait.[1]

Because Russia maintains an array of nonmilitary instruments of power in the Black Sea region that it could employ to undermine unity around a military initiative, engagement on regional security will necessarily extend beyond the military realm. In light of the potential avenues for influence that the new TurkStream pipeline might create in Turkey, and potentially Bulgaria, robust energy dialogues with both

---

[1] Timothy M. Bonds et al., *What Role Can Land-Based, Multi-Domain Anti-Access/Area Denial Forces Play in Deterring or Defeating Aggression?* Santa Monica, Calif.: RAND Corporation, RR-1820-A, 2017, p. 95.

countries on their gas hub aspirations could identify options to maximize regional interconnectors and alternative sources of gas, such as that provided through the Trans-Anatolian Natural Gas Pipeline, as well as future Romanian Black Sea gas extraction. An open-source initiative to highlight streams of Russian government investment in the region could complement existing public analyses of Russian military power and help to guide dialogues with regional leaders.[2] In particular, diplomatic engagement on Russian funding for media outlets in the Black Sea—and investment in alternatives—could address a primary vehicle for Russian influence operations in the region. Finally, targeted senior-level political discussions could seek to encourage a regionally driven approach by improving communication about areas of commonality and divergence regarding threat perceptions, identifying potential contingencies, and evaluating mitigation measures before a crisis.

---

[2]   For example, see U.S. Defense Intelligence Agency, *Russia Military Power: Building a Military to Support Great Power Aspirations*, Washington, D.C., 2017.

Acknowledgments

I am indebted to several RAND colleagues who contributed their time and intellect to this project. In particular, Steve Flanagan generously shared his extensive regional expertise and sound guidance at every phase of the project in his capacity as senior adviser. Elizabeth Bartels contributed methodological advice and support to the game design process, facilitation skills during the course of the game, and important contributions to postgame data analysis, including the generation of Figures 4.2 and 4.3. RAND Navy fellow CDR T. J. Gilmore shared his naval expertise and experience throughout the project. Rebecca Wasser skillfully facilitated the game's Russia team and offered methodological feedback on game design. Note takers Abby Fanlo, Leah Hershey, and Sunni Bhatt provided excellent written summaries of the event that served as a basis for report analysis. RAND colleagues Clint Reach, Catherine Dale, and Andrew Radin participated in the June 2018 game and offered helpful feedback. I am particularly grateful to the leadership team of the RAND National Defense Research Institute for their sponsorship of this project with internal funding, and in particular to former deputy director Christopher Chivvis for his excellent advice, support, and encouragement. Thank you to reviewers Dimitar Bechev and Irina Chindea for their improvements to the final report.

Abbreviations

A2AD	anti-access/area denial
ASCM	antiship cruise missile
EEZ	exclusive economic zone
LACM	land attack cruise missile
NAC	North Atlantic Council of NATO
NATO	North Atlantic Treaty Organization
SAM	surface-to-air missile
SRBM	short-range ballistic missile

CHAPTER ONE

Introduction

The Black Sea region represents a potential flashpoint for Russia and the West. As the site of two Russian ground combat operations, in 2008 and 2014, and a critical transit area for Russian maritime access to Syria, the security environment has declined for the three North Atlantic Treaty Organization (NATO) allies and two partners bordering the sea. The November 25, 2018, seizure of three Ukrainian vessels by the Russian navy in the Kerch Strait stands as the most recent reminder of the potential for military confrontation in a region in which the military balance of power has increasingly tipped against U.S. allies and partners.[1] Several factors have contributed to this trend, including Russia's seizure of Crimea in 2014, as well as the expansion and modernization of Russia's Black Sea Fleet since 2014 to include new cruise-missile-capable diesel submarines and frigates, deployments

---

[1] See F. Stephen Larrabee and Stephen J. Flanagan, "The Growing Importance of Black Sea Security," *U.S. News and World Report,* July 11, 2016. The Stockholm International Peace Research Institute similarly highlights the military buildup in the Black Sea region and conflict potential, including the "danger of unintended clashes through military accidents and incidents, and due to unpredictable escalations and the potential for conflict spillover." Neil Melvin, *Rebuilding Collective Security in the Black Sea*, Solna, Sweden: Stockholm International Peace Research Institute, SIPRI Policy Paper 50, December 2018. See also Jakob Hedenskog, Erika Holmquist, and Johan Norberg, *Security in the Caucasus: Russian Policy and Military Posture*, Stockholm: Swedish Defence Research Agency, 2018, which concludes that Russia's military posture in the Caucasus is overdimensioned and is designed for a potential large-scale conflict in the southern war theater, including the wider Middle East, rather than just local conflicts in the region.

of air and coastal defense assets to Crimea, and deployment of additional ground troops to the Southern Military District.[2]

Although Western forces have responded with steps to assert presence, including NATO's tailored forward presence, increased periodic visits by U.S. vessels, and bolstered participation in region-led exercises, any major effort to further enhance defense and deterrence activities in the Black Sea would require the consent—and ideally participation—of regional allies and partners. A RAND national security game and associated research suggest, however, that even if the United States were fully committed to promoting a regional coalition initiative to further enhance deterrent presence in the Black Sea, it could be difficult to develop and sustain consensus over a response.

Approach: A RAND Black Sea Game

To assess these political and military challenges more systematically, RAND developed and conducted a national security game to consider regional military responses to a notional future security crisis. The project began with literature-based research on the emerging military balance in the Black Sea, as well as the potential levers of nonmilitary influence that Russia might bring to bear on the decisionmaking of littoral allies and partners. This research identified relevant trends and issues to be explored in the game. The research was also more directly applied to game development in order to create a game scenario, a set of potential Western military responses, and a deck of cards offered to the Russia team representing potential targeted actions to influence each of the other regional teams.

Extrapolating from trends identified in the research phase of the project, RAND developed a fictional scenario to explore how a crisis might play out. The scenario included Russian defense of an expanded exclusive economic zone (EEZ), harassment of Romanian workers on offshore oil rigs, and a fatal incident stemming from aggressive Russian

---

[2] Dmitry Gorenburg, "Is a New Russian Black Sea Fleet Coming? Or Is It Here?" *War on the Rocks*, July 31, 2018.

Su-24 bomber tactics. The fictional events served as the centerpiece for a June 2018 game convening policy experts and practitioners from the United States and the Black Sea region. Participants playing the United States and seven regional allies and partners—Romania, Bulgaria, Turkey, Georgia, Ukraine, Moldova, and Greece—were tasked with weighing a set of proposed response initiatives to more effectively deter and defend against Black Sea security challenges, set in a time frame between 2020 and 2025. The notional establishment of a Black Sea task force served as a centerpiece for decisionmaking. Participants composing Team Russia were asked to develop a strategic assessment and strategize about what political, military, and economic levers they could apply to influence the other regional players. RAND presented the Russia team with a deck of research-based cards representing potential military, economic, or political actions of the Russian government that the team could choose to discard, change, or play. During the two-round game, the Russia team then played its selected cards against other regional teams as the regional teams deliberated about their roles in an enhanced military response.

Report Structure

This report is organized into five chapters. Chapter Two presents research findings on the evolving Russian military presence in the Black Sea and Western military responses to date. Chapter Three reviews the sometimes-complex relationships between Russia and the five littoral Black Sea states, Turkey, Romania, Bulgaria, Ukraine, and Georgia, and identifies potential sources of Russian political and economic leverage. Chapter Four offers details on game mechanics and presents insights from the June 2018 event. Finally, Chapter Five offers conclusions derived from the research and game components of the projects, as well as recommendations for policymakers.

CHAPTER TWO

The New Black Sea Military Balance

In recent years, the Black Sea has become a primary locus of Russian military activity. Russia has repeatedly demonstrated a proclivity for applying military force to protect and advance interests in the region, as evidenced by Russian ground incursions into the sovereign territories of two regional U.S. partners, use of the Black Sea Fleet and other capabilities for power projection into operations in Syria and the broader Mediterranean, and increasingly muscular efforts to dominate the Sea of Azov.[1] Close encounters between Russian aircraft and U.S. naval vessels in the Black Sea appear to indicate Russian willingness to take on potential military risk to signal a sphere of influence.[2] Russia has also prioritized investment in its regional military posture, including through the modernization of the Black Sea Fleet, deployments of access denial assets, and deployment of additional ground troops to the Southern Military District. As a result of these developments, the Black Sea is now one of the most militarily active regions in Europe. If a regional confrontation were ever to escalate, Russia's new Black Sea capabilities and force posture could impose significant operational constraints on a NATO alliance or coalition military response.

External naval military presence in the Black Sea is legally constrained by the 1936 Montreux Convention, implemented by Turkey. According to the convention, nonlittoral states are limited to 21 days in the Black Sea, with a maximum aggregate weight of 45,000 tons

---

[1] Glen Grant, "Real Action Is Now Needed in the Azov Sea," *Kyiv Post*, August 20, 2018.

[2] Sam LaGrone, "USS *Porter* Buzzed by Russian Planes in Black Sea," *USNI News*, February 14, 2017.

for military naval presence.[3] The Turkish government interprets the convention as prohibiting aircraft carriers from passing through the Dardanelle Straits, and submarine traffic is limited to littoral states transiting for repair or construction.[4] Turkey requires prior notice of transit and retains freedom of choice over the application of the convention: Turkey can invite a naval force of any tonnage or composition for a port visit, and during wartime the passage of warships is left to the discretion of the Turkish government.[5]

Increased Russian Military Investment and Geographic Advantage

The Russian government appears to be actively seeking to signal its military capability in the Black Sea. In September 2016, before a visit to Turkey, Russian chief of general staff Valery Gerasimov announced that "everything is different" for the Black Sea military balance, claiming that Russia's Black Sea Fleet could now "destroy a potential enemy's amphibious force on the way, starting from the ports of embarkation."[6] Several weeks later, a Russian government-owned news

---

[3] This includes a maximum of 30,000 tons for any single nonlittoral state. Convention Regarding the Regime of the Straits, signed in Montreux, Switzerland, July 20, 1936.

[4] "Implementation of the Montreux Convention," Turkish Ministry of Foreign Affairs, undated; Convention Regarding the Regime, Article 12.

[5] Article 17 of the Montreux Convention states that "nothing in the provisions of the preceding Articles shall prevent a naval force of any tonnage or composition from paying a courtesy visit of limited duration to a port in the Straits, at the invitation of the Turkish Government." Article 20 of the convention states that "in time of war, Turkey being belligerent, the provisions of Articles 10 to 18 shall not be applicable; the passage of warships shall be left entirely to the discretion of the Turkish Government." "Convention Regarding the Regime of the Straits," *American Journal of International Law*, Vol. 31, No. 1, 1937, pp. 1–18.

[6] General Valery Gerasimov announced that "several years ago the capability of the [Russian] fleet was sharply contrasted, in particular, with the Turkish navy, when it was said that Turkey is virtually the master of the Black Sea. Now everything is different." Joshua Kucera, "Russia Claims 'Mastery' over Turkey in Black Sea," *Eurasianet*, September 25, 2016b. He further stated that "the Black Sea Fleet has all essential means of reconnaissance capable of identifying targets as far as 500 kilometers away and means of attack." Bleda Kurtdarcan and Barın Kayaoğlu, "Russia, Turkey and the Black Sea A2/AD Arms Race," *National Interest*, March 5, 2017.

outlet similarly observed that "Sevastopol Bay creates unique opportunities for Moscow. Together with the new base in Novorossiysk, Russia can fully control the Bosphorus, the military infrastructure in Bulgaria and can neutralize the threat posed by the U.S. missile defense base in Romania."[7] Statements such as these may represent a warning, but they are also largely accurate.

Recent Russian naval modernization prioritizing the Black Sea has transformed a formerly anemic Black Sea Fleet into a more formidable force.[8] Figure 2.1 highlights changes to Russia's Black Sea naval inventory between 2010 and 2018. The buildup of the fleet was cited as one of the Kremlin's most significant national defense investment priorities for its State Armament Program for 2011–2020.[9] The effort has yielded additional vessels with new capabilities, including six new corvettes and six new *Kilo*-class submarines, all equipped with the Kalibr family of missiles, which includes the 3M-54 (SS-N-27) antiship cruise missile and the 3M-14 (SS-N-30) land attack cruise missile.[10] The fleet's three new *Admiral Grigorovich*–class missile frigates can also mount Kalibrs along with Shtil air defense missiles, as well as antisubmarine torpedoes and rocket launchers.[11]

Investments in stealth technologies have permitted Russian diesel and battery-powered submarines to move more quietly in the water. Applying the new Russian submarine challenge to the North Atlantic passage between Greenland, Iceland, and the United Kingdom, a 2017 tabletop exercise performed by the Center for New American Security

---

[7] Nikolai Litovkin, "'Black Hole': What Makes Russia's Newest Submarine Unique?" *Russia Beyond the Headlines*, November 29, 2016.

[8] Dmitry Boltenkov, ed., *Russia's New Army*, Moscow: Center for Analysis of Strategies and Technologies, 2011; Igor Delanoe, "After the Crimean Crisis: Towards a Greater Russian Maritime Power in the Black Sea," *Southeast European and Black Sea Studies*, Vol. 14, No. 13, 2014, pp. 367–382. See also Gorenburg, 2018; U.S. Defense Intelligence Agency, 2017, p. 67.

[9] Boltenkov, *Russia's New Army*, cited in Delanoe, 2014.

[10] Dmitry Gorenburg, "Black Sea Fleet Projects Power Westwards," *Oxford Analytica*, April 2016a. Gorenburg notes that 3M-14 cruise missiles can put at risk land targets at ranges of up to 2,500 km (1,600 m).

[11] The land attack version of Kalibr has a claimed range of 2,600 km; the antiship version has a claimed range of 300 km. Sebastien Roblin, "Introducing Russia's 5 Deadliest Warships in the Black Sea," *National Interest*, December 1, 2018.

Figure 2.1
Expansion of Russia's Black Sea Fleet, 2010–2018

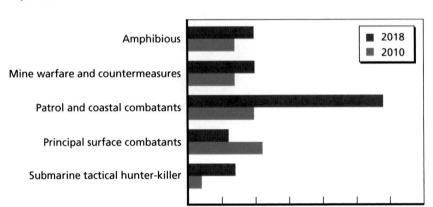

SOURCES: International Institute for Strategic Studies, *The Military Balance 2010*, London: Routledge for the International Institute for Strategic Studies, 2010; International Institute for Strategic Studies, *The Military Balance 2018*, London: Routledge for the International Institute for Strategic Studies, 2018.

concluded that the United States is "nowhere near ready to respond quickly to undersea challenges" from Russia.[12] Closer to the Black Sea, the U.S. Navy has had to contend with new challenges as it seeks to track Russian submarines conducting cruise missile strikes on Syria from the Mediterranean.[13] The passage of Russia's Black Sea submarines could potentially be constrained by Turkey under the Montreux Convention. Currently, Montreux places operational restrictions on Russia's submarine presence at Tartus: while the submarines are permitted to return to the Black Sea for repairs, Turkey is not required under Montreux to allow submarines to return to the Mediterranean through the straits.[14]

---

[12] Julianne Smith and Jerry Hendrix, *Forgotten Waters: Minding the GIUK Gap*, tabletop exercise report, Washington, D.C.: Center for New American Security, May 2, 2017, p. 7.

[13] Julian Barnes, "A Russian Ghost Submarine, Its U.S. Pursuers and a Deadly New Cold War," *Wall Street Journal*, October 20, 2017.

[14] Dave Majumdar, "All Is Not Well with Russia's Black Sea Fleet," *National Interest*, June 20, 2018. Majumdar cites Article 12 of the Montreux Convention. For the text of Article 12, see "Convention Regarding the Regime," p. 5.

New geographic realities, including Russian territorial control of Crimea, have further altered the regional security landscape.[15] In March 2014, the Kremlin indicated its intent to "fully utilize the geostrategic potential of Crimea."[16] The following March, President Vladimir Putin ordered nuclear bomber jets to be temporarily deployed in Crimea.[17] Since its intervention in Crimea, Russia has nearly doubled the number of service personnel on the peninsula and implemented a nearly sevenfold increase in tanks, combat armored vehicles, and artillery systems.[18] By 2017, Russian military personnel on the peninsula numbered at about 28,000, including naval personnel associated with the Black Sea Fleet.[19] After the intervention, Russia claimed that lease agreements prohibiting the basing of new Russian ships in Crimea were rendered obsolete, paving the way for unfettered use of the peninsula.[20]

Since that time, Russia has used Crimea as a base to project maritime power into the Mediterranean and to improve its degree of geographic control over Black Sea.[21] As indicated by the November 2018 seizure of Ukrainian vessels in the Kerch Strait, Russia has used its new geographic position to enforce a more aggressive Russian naval posture that could ultimately choke Ukrainian commercial interests in the Sea of Azov.[22] Before the incident, Russia had transferred two

---

[15] Gorenburg, 2018. See also Dimitar Bechev, *Rival Power: Russia in Southeast Europe*, New Haven, Conn.: Yale University Press, 2017, p. 184. See also Alex Schneider, "Russia's Black Sea Fleet Buildup" *The Maritime Executive*, March 29 2017.

[16] Akin Uver, "Ankara to Black Sea: Turkey and Russia's Age-Old Struggle for Regional Supremacy," *Foreign Affairs*, May 12, 2014.

[17] "Russia Expands Military Exercises to 80,000 Troops," Agence France-Presse, March 19, 2015.

[18] Deborah Sanders, "Rebuilding the Ukrainian Navy," *Naval War College Review*, Vol. 70, No. 4, 2017, pp. 61–77.

[19] Alexandra Kuimova and Seimon T. Wezeman, *Russia and Black Sea Security*, SIPRI Background Paper, Solna, Sweden: Stockholm International Peace Research Institute, December 2018b.

[20] Dmitry Gorenburg, "Black Sea Fleet Projects Power Westwards," *Russian Military Reform* blog, July 20, 2016b.

[21] Gorenburg, 2016b.

[22] This point is made in Grant, 2018.

Project 1204 *Shmel*-class gunboats and a Project 1400M *Zhuk* patrol craft from its Caspian Flotilla to the Azov Sea.[23] Despite a 2003 legal agreement between Ukraine and Russia dictating passage through the Kerch Strait, Russia claims that its control of both sides of the strait since 2014 has created legal ambiguities around Ukrainian navigation rights.[24] The incident has been compared to the "creeping annexation" associated with the shifting of "borders" between Georgia and its breakaway province of South Ossetia.[25]

Russia's assertion of maritime power in the Black Sea and beyond has been improved in part by the development of extensive radar stations on Crimean hilltops.[26] A Russian radar regiment in Sevastopol and a Murmansk-BN coastal electronic warfare complex may provide, according to Russian government-controlled media claims, the capacity to monitor NATO vessels across the Black Sea and Mediterranean.[27] During a military confrontation, these capabilities could prove an integral part of Russian efforts to enforce an antiaccess/area denial (A2AD) zone across the region.[28]

Russia has also deployed additional air and air defense assets on the peninsula. Following the 2014 intervention, Russia rehabilitated abandoned Ukrainian airfields and expanded its previously based naval aviation unit in Crimea to include 12 new Su-30SMs, as well as Ka-52 and Mi-28N helicopters.[29] The Black Sea Fleet's independent mixed aircraft regiment includes Be-12, An-26, and KA-27 air-

---

[23] Bruce Jones, "Ukraine Reinforces Its Presence in Azov Sea," *Jane's Navy International*, September 13, 2018.

[24] David B. Larter and Matthew Bodner, "The Sea of Azov Won't Become the New South China Sea (and Russia Knows It)," *Defense News*, November 28, 2018.

[25] Nona Mikhelidze and Nathalie Tocci, "Europe's Russia Sanctions Are Not Working," *Politico*, November 28, 2018.

[26] "In Crimea, Russia Signals Military Resolve with New and Revamped Bases," Reuters, November 1, 2016.

[27] Ruslan Minich, "Russia Shows Its Military Might in the Black Sea and Beyond," *Ukraine-Alert* (Atlantic Council blog), November 6, 2018.

[28] Minich, 2018.

[29] Gorenburg, 2018; "In Crimea," 2016.

craft.[30] In March 2019, Russian defense officials announced that they were deploying "squadrons" of Tupolev Tu-22M3 Backfire bombers—which may be upgraded to carry Kh-32 long-range cruise missiles—to Crimea in response to NATO missile defense installations in Poland and Romania.[31] After 2014, Russian aircraft became more active across Europe, flying near NATO countries in groups and often with their transponders off. Overall, NATO reported that alliance pilots had conducted over 100 intercepts of Russian aircraft in the year following Russia's intervention in Crimea, about three times the number of intercepts in 2013.[32]

Land-based missile systems complement the air- and sea-launched missiles previously mentioned. Following its 2008 operations in Georgia, the Russian military announced the deployment of Russian S-300 air defense missiles to Georgia's breakaway province of Abkhazia.[33] In 2015, President Putin announced the placement of Bastion mobile coastal defense missile systems in Crimea, as well as S-400 Triumph air defense systems.[34] Russia reportedly planned to deploy additional Bastion battalions in 2019.[35] Russia's coastal systems in Crimea also include the shorter-range Bal system with Kh-35U missiles.[36] As early as 2014, NATO's former Supreme Allied Commander Europe, General Philip Breedlove, voiced concerns that the militarization of Crimea, which included cruise and surface-to-air missiles, would "bring an

---

[30] Minich, 2018.

[31] Sam LaGrone, "Russians Use U.S. Navy's Aegis Ashore as Excuse to Deploy Strategic Bombers to Crimea," *USNI News*, March 18, 2019; "Meet Russia's Tu-22M3 Backfire, the Bomber That Could Sink a Navy Aircraft Carrier," *National Interest*, June 5, 2018.

[32] Jamie Dettmer, "NATO Commander Warns of Crimea 'Militarization,'" *Voice of America*, November 26, 2014.

[33] "Russian General Says Kremlin Deploys Air-Defense Missiles in Abkhazia," *Radio Free Europe/Radio Liberty*, August 11, 2010.

[34] Kurtdarcan and Kayaoğlu, 2017.

[35] "Russia to Reinforce Black Sea Fleet with Bastion Missile Systems," *UAWire*, March 4, 2019.

[36] Kuimova and Wezeman, 2018b.

effect on almost the entire Black Sea."[37] By 2015, General Breedlove warned that "Russia has developed a very strong A2/AD capability in the Black Sea," noting that Russian antiship cruise missiles could now cover the entire Back Sea, while defensive missile systems cover 40–50 percent of the Black Sea.[38] The Russian government has similarly claimed that its missile defense systems across the region—combined with ship-based platforms—can deny access to much, if not all, of the Black Sea during a conflict.[39] Notably, the precise ranges of Russian missile systems have been disputed by some analysts, potentially making the A2AD "bubble" less effective against fighter jets and low-altitude cruise missiles.[40] Table 2.1 presents key Russian missile systems and their reported ranges in the Black Sea region.

In addition to bolstering maritime and air defense presence, Russia has also expanded its ground forces in the Black Sea region. In 2016, it announced the establishment of a new combined arms army (the 8th) within the Southern Military District. In late 2018, the 150th Motorized Division—a central component of the district's ground presence—activated its second motorized rifle regiment, which would complete the division's operational strength of two tank regiments and two motorized rifle regiments.[41] After 2008, Russia established land bases in Abkhazia (7th Military Base) and South Ossetia

---

[37] Quoted in Dettmer, 2014.

[38] Quoted in Thomas Gibbons-Neff, "Top NATO General: Russians Starting to Build Air Defense Bubble over Syria," *Washington Post*, September 29, 2015.

[39] "General Staff: Russia-Turkey Balance of Force in Black Sea Has Changed over Years," TASS, September 14, 2016.

[40] The Swedish Defence Research Agency, for example, assesses that "in its current configuration, the S-400 system should mainly be considered a threat to large high-value aircraft such as AWACS [Airborne Warning and Control System] or transport aircraft at medium to high altitudes, out to a range of 200–250 km. In contrast, the effective range against agile fighter jets and cruise missiles operating at low altitudes can be as little 20–35 km." Robert Dalsjo, Christofer Berglund, and Michael Jonsson, *Bursting the Bubble: Russian A2/AD in the Baltic Sea Region: Capabilities, Countermeasures, and Implications*, Stockholm: Swedish Defence Research Agency, March 2019, p. 10.

[41] Samuel Cranny-Evans, "Russia's Southern Military District Receives Mechanized, Airmobile Reinforcements," *Jane's Defence Weekly*, December 5, 2018.

Table 2.1
Key Russian Missile Systems and Reported Ranges in the Black Sea

Missile	Class	Reported Range	Peacetime Location
9K720 *Iskander* (SS-26 STONE)	SRBM	400–500 km	Krasnodar, Rostov-on-the-Don
S-400 *Triumf* (SA-21 GROWLER)	SAM	150–400 km	Crimea, Abkhazia
P-800 *Oniks* (SS-N-26 STROBILE) 3K55 *Bastion-P* (SSC-5 STOOGE)	Ship-launched ASCM Ground-launched ASCM	300 km	Crimea
3M-14 *Kalibr* (SS-N-30A)	LACM	1,500–2,500 km	Corvettes; submarines
3M-54 *Kalibr* (SS-N-27 SIZZLER)	ASCM	220 km (3M54) 300 km (3M54M1)	*Admiral Grigorovich*-class frigate
9K317 *Buk-M2* (SA-17 GRIZZLY) 3S90M *Shtil-1* (SA-N-7 GOLLUM)	Ground-launched SAM Ship-launched SAM	50 km	Crimea, *Admiral Grigorovich*-class frigate
3K60 *Bal* (SSC-6 SENNIGHT)	Ground-launched ASCM	120 km	Crimea

NOTES: Data as of June 2019. ASCM = antiship cruise missile; LACM = land attack cruise missile; SAM = surface-to-air missile; SRBM = short-range ballistic missile.

(4th Military Base). Georgian sources indicate that some 4,000 Russian troops occupy the former, and another 4,000 occupy the latter.[42] Russia's "peacekeeping" ground presence in the Moldovan breakaway republic of Transnistria—between 1,500 and 2,000 troops—increased the number of exercises from 48 in 2016 to over 150 in 2018 and expanded the scope to large-scale events, including practicing the crossing of the Dneister toward Moldova.[43]

---

[42] Giorgi Menabde, "Russian Military Absorbs 'Army of South Ossetia,'" *Eurasia Daily Monitor*, March 21, 2017; David Batashvili, "Russia Troop Deployments Menace Georgia," *Civil.ge*, April 4, 2017.

[43] Heather Conley and Donatienne Ruy, "Kremlin Playbook: Spotlight Moldova," *Center for Strategic and International Studies*, July 19, 2018.

Western Military Responses

While the Western military response to Russia's 2008 intervention in Georgia was muted, NATO allies and partners have undertaken some military steps to deter further aggressions since Russia's 2014 invasion of Crimea and military intervention in eastern Ukraine. At the 2016 Warsaw Summit, the alliance initiated a Tailored Forward Presence in Romania and Bulgaria that, in addition to signaling resolve, could help ensure that troops already on the ground would help reduce the need to conduct a forced entry in an antiaccess, area denial setting.[44] The alliance's regional presence includes a new multinational division headquarters and a Romanian-led framework land brigade, as well as enhanced training, periodic maritime visits and exercises, and regional air policing.[45] NATO has also strengthened its partnership with Georgia, including through the 2014 adoption of the Substantial NATO-Georgia Package to provide NATO support for Georgian defense and interoperability in 14 areas, including strategic and operational planning, acquisition and procurement, aviation, air defense, and maritime security.[46]

NATO's post-Crimea initiatives did not extend as far as some governments in the region had hoped. Black Sea allies did not receive combat forces training or staff units, and NATO's regional combat force presence remained noncontinuous.[47] Before the 2016 Warsaw Summit, Romania floated a proposal for a permanent NATO mari-

---

[44] David Vergun, "U.S. Soldiers in Bulgaria, Romania Deter Aggression, Assure Allies," *Army News Service*, September 26, 2017.

[45] "The Black Sea Region: A Critical Intersection," *NATO Review*, May 25, 2018. See also Boris Toucas, "NATO and Russia in the Black Sea: A New Confrontation?" *Center for Strategic and International Studies*, March 6, 2017.

[46] Alexandra Kuimova and Seimon T. Wezeman, *Georgia and Black Sea Security*, SIPRI Background Paper, Solna, Sweden: Stockholm International Peace Research Institute, December 2018a. Enhanced cooperation between Georgia and NATO is also noted in Deborah Sanders, "The Crimean Crisis and Russia's Maritime Power in the Black Sea," *Defence-in-Depth* blog, October 27, 2014.

[47] Iulia-Sabina Joja, "Dealing with the Russian Lake Next Door: Romania and Black Sea Security," *War on the Rocks*, August 15, 2018.

time presence in the Black Sea, alternatively referred to as a "NATO Black Sea Fleet" or a permanent "flotilla." The presence would consist of vessels from littoral navies, as well as rotating ships from other NATO navies, including those of Germany, Italy, and the United States.[48] Turkey and Bulgaria initially supported the initiative, but a day after Russia warned against the initiative, the Bulgarian government announced that it would not participate.[49]

With three treaty allies and two major partners on the periphery, the United States has also responded bilaterally to allied requests to bolster its periodic maritime presence and participation in regional exercises. In 2018, the United States' periodic presence in the Black Sea included deployments of guided-missile destroyers, a *Ticonderoga*-class guided-missile cruiser, and an expeditionary fast transport ship.[50] The United States has continued its leadership role in the annual multinational Sea Breeze exercise, which in 2018 for the first time incorporated embarkment on the command-and-control ship USS *Mount Whitney*, as well as the participation of U.S. P-8 Poseidon maritime patrol aircraft.[51] The 2018 Sea Breeze exercise also included 50 U.S. Marines and involved company-size mechanized attacks.[52] A partnership between Ukraine and the California National Guard expanded to include California National Air Guard contributions to a large, Ukrainian-hosted multinational air exercise that included close air support missions, cyber defense operations, and air sovereignty defense.[53]

---

[48] Joshua Kucera, "Romania Pushing for Permanent NATO Presence in Black Sea," *Eurasianet*, January 18, 2016a.

[49] "Bulgaria Says Will Not Join Any NATO Black Sea Fleet After Russian Warning," *Reuters*, June 16, 2016.

[50] Kyle Rempfer, "Here's the US Military Footprint in the Black Sea Region," *Military Times*, November 27, 2018a.

[51] Ryan Browne, "US Show of Force Sends Russia a Message in Black Sea," *CNN*, February 20, 2018; Megan Eckstein, "U.S. Navy Command Ship, Destroyer in Black Sea for Annual Sea Breeze Exercise," *USNI News*, July 10, 2018.

[52] Rempfer, 2018a.

[53] Rempfer, 2018a.

U.S. presence at Romania's Mihail Kogalniceanu Air Base and Bulgaria's Novo Selo training base has expanded since Russia's 2014 incursion into Ukraine. Since 2015, one battalion from the rotating U.S. Army armored brigade combat team in Europe is placed at Mihail Kogalniceanu, and two companies from the combat team are at Novo Selo.[54] Mihail Kogalniceanu, described by former U.S. Army Europe commanding general LTG Ben Hodges as "a hub, a power projection platform out into the Black Sea for air and land forces," also has the capacity to conduct maintenance, store ammunition, and host a larger mission command element.[55] Until September 2018, the U.S. Marine Corps had operated from the base as part of the Black Sea Rotational Force.[56] The U.S. 2019 defense budget includes about $27 million for infrastructure modernization and construction in Romania and Bulgaria.[57] Since this research was conducted in 2018 and early 2019, the United States has taken some steps to further bolster its presence in the region. The 2021 National Defense Authorization Act included a request for $130.5 million for major upgrades to Campia Turzii Air Base in central Romania, and in 2019, USAFE deployed MQ-9 Reaper drones to the site on a temporary rotation.[58] Additionally, in July 2020, U.S. Secretary of Defense Mark Esper announced the U.S. intent to deploy a Stryker brigade to Romania as part of ongoing changes in the U.S. defense posture in Europe.

In response to the November 2018 Kerch Strait incident, the United States flew increased military observation missions and deployed the USS *Fort McHenry* to participate in joint sea maneuvers with a Romanian frigate in territorial and international Black Sea

---

[54] Kyle Rempfer, "Why Russia Is Swallowing the Black Sea and Won't Stop Until It Has 'Choked Out Ukraine,'" *Military Times*, December 31, 2018b.

[55] Rempfer, 2018b.

[56] Shawn Snow, "No More Marine Rotations to the Black Sea. The Corps Is Focusing Here Instead," *Marine Corps Times*, November 29, 2018.

[57] Ana Maria Luca, "US Plans to Upgrade Military Bases in Romania, Bulgaria," *Balkan Insight*, August 15, 2018.

[58] John Vandiver, "Air Force Wants to Turn Soviet-Era Base in Romania into NATO Black Sea Hub," *Stars and Stripes*, July 9, 2020.

waters.[59] A U.S. Navy destroyer also conducted freedom-of-navigation operations in contested waters in the Sea of Japan, near the Russian port city of Vladivostok.[60] The United States also increased its maritime security assistance to Ukraine. In December 2018, highlighting Russia's "dangerous escalation and unjustified November 25 attack," the U.S. State Department announced a $10 million investment in foreign military financing to support the development of Ukrainian naval capabilities.[61] More recently, a $250 million aid package was approved by the U.S. Congress in June 2020, supporting Ukrainian maritime and air situational awareness; naval capabilities command and control; cyber defense; counter artillery; medical treatment and MEDEVAC; counter disinformation efforts; and training and education, according to media reports.[62]

Russian defense spending on the Black Sea Fleet has prompted increased naval investment from other littoral states as well. Romania, in particular, has embarked on an extensive military procurement, modernization, and expansion plan for 2017–2026, increasing defense spending by 50 percent to $4 billion in 2017, the largest relative increase in the world.[63] Analysts have described Romania's procurement objectives as twofold: large-scale procurement of military equipment and knowledge transfer to help rebuild Romanian industry.[64] It has also announced plans for the procurement of three new submarines. The

---

[59] Zachary Cohen and Ryan Browne, "US Military Flexes Muscles in Message to Russia," *CNN*, December 6, 2018; "U.S. Warship Arrives at Romanian Port amid Black Sea Tensions," *Radio Free Europe/Radio Liberty*, January 8, 2019.

[60] Ankit Panda, "US Navy Conducts First Post–Cold War FONOP in Peter the Great Bay, Off Russian Coast," *The Diplomat*, December 6, 2018.

[61] "After Calls for Black Sea FONOPS, US to Support Ukraine Navy with $10m Investment," *Naval Today*, December 24, 2018.

[62] Howard Altman, "$250 Million Aid Package to Ukraine Will Support US Security Too, Defense Experts Say," *Military Times*, June 12, 2020.

[63] Sorin Melenciuc, "Romania's Military Spending Rose 50 pct to USD 4 bln in 2017, the Biggest Increase in the World," *Business Review*, March 5, 2018; Nan Tian et al., *Trends in World Military Expenditure, 2017*, fact sheet, Solna, Sweden: Stockholm International Peace Research Institute, May 2018.

[64] Joja, 2018.

Romanian government announced in March 2019 the final phase of a $150 million tender to acquire anti-ship missile systems in the Black Sea.[65] In July 2019, the Romanian government announced an intent to purchase four new Gowind corvettes from France's Naval Group and Romanian partner Santierul Naval Constanta in a $1.3 billion deal that would also upgrade two frigates and construct a local maintenance facility and training center.[66]

Romania's Ministry of Defense has also invested in land and air forces and capabilities, including a $1-billion deal in 2018 for 227 Piranha V infantry fighting vehicles for Romanian ground forces.[67] In 2017 and 2018, the Romanian government signed deals with the U.S. Army to purchase ten Patriot air and missile defense systems, and in early 2018 it signed a letter of agreement to purchase U.S.-built High Mobility Artillery Rocket Systems and Guided Multiple Launch Rocket Systems.[68] In January 2018, Romania intensified its military cooperation with neighboring Moldova with an announcement of plans for a joint battalion for emergency situations and resumption of bilateral military drills to improve interoperability.[69]

Bulgarian defense expenditures rose marginally in 2017 to $1.5 billion, as Bulgaria began to implement the development plan it set out in 2015.[70] An earlier naval modernization program, which began in 2005, resulted in the procurement in 2008 and 2009 of two

---

[65] Jaroslaw Adamoski, "Saab, Diehl Defence Team Up to Offer Missile to Romanian, Bulgarian Navies," *Defense News*, September 4, 2019.

[66] Jaroslaw Adamoski, "Romania, Bulgaria Boost Defense Buys Amid Fear of Russia," *Defense News*, September 8, 2019.

[67] Jaroslaw Adamowski, "Romania Inks $1B Deal for Hundreds of Infantry Fighting Vehicles," *Defense News*, January 12, 2018a.

[68] Tauren Dyson, "Raytheon to Supply Romania with Missile Defense Systems," *UPI*, November 4, 2018; Jen Judson, "Romania Signs Off on US Deal to Become First European HIMARS Customer," *Defense News*, February 28, 2018.

[69] Madalin Necsutu, "Moldova, Romania Boost Military Cooperation with Joint Battalion," *Balkan Insight*, February 6, 2018.

[70] International Institute for Strategic Studies, 2018, p. 88.

Wielingen-class frigates and one *Tripartite*-class mine hunter from the Belgian Navy.[71] Bulgaria has also embarked on a series of military-modernization projects that—even when approved—may be deferred until as late as 2029 to reduce budgetary impact.[72] In 2016, the Bulgarian government approved a $1.4-billion purchase program to invest in upgraded air and naval assets, including the purchase of two modern corvettes and 16 fixed-wing tactical aircraft and the modernization of 10 Mig-29 fighter jets.[73] In January 2019, the Bulgarian government initiated negotiations with the United States on the purchase of eight new F-16V fighter jets to replace their MiG-29s and move closer to NATO standards. If finalized, the deal would be Bulgaria's largest ever military procurement.[74]

Ukraine lost over 60 percent of its navy in Russia's Crimea takeover, including major warships, its most modern naval platforms, and its Crimea-based Black Sea headquarters facilities, which included much of its naval signals intelligence, training, administration, maintenance, and logistics infrastructure.[75] Additionally, about 75 percent of Ukraine's maritime personnel remained in Crimea after the Russian takeover.[76] Despite these setbacks, and facing significant budgetary challenges, Ukraine has since sought to rebuild some capabilities, prioritizing the acquisition of smaller, faster, less expensive platforms— "a mosquito fleet"—to protect Ukrainian coastlines.[77] In September 2018, Ukraine's National Security and Defense Council approved

---

[71] George Tsiboukis, "Bulgarian Navy Corvette Procurement Is Back On," *Defense IQ*, October 2, 2017.

[72] International Institute for Strategic Studies, 2018, p. 88.

[73] Michael Peterson, "The Naval Power Shift in the Black Sea," *War on the Rocks*, January 9, 2019; Carlo Munoz, "Bulgaria Approves $1.4 Billion for New Warships, Fighters," *UPI*, April 5, 2016.

[74] "Bulgaria to Buy Eight New F-16s from US," *Emerging Europe*, January 10, 2019.

[75] Sanders, 2017. Sanders, 2017, p. 6, writes that "in total, the service lost eleven ships and boats, eight auxiliary vessels, and its only submarine."

[76] Sanders, 2017.

[77] Sanders, 2017.

measures to reinforce Ukraine's southern military presence, including in the Sea of Azov. These measures included a missile-equipped naval infantry group, the relocation of Ukraine's southern and second-largest naval base and associated battalion of naval vessels from the Black Sea port of Mykolaiv to the Azov Sea port of Berdyansk, and the transfer of three Project 58155 *Gyurza-M* armored gun boats to Berdyansk.[78] In September 2018, the United States transferred two Coast Guard patrol craft to the Ukrainian Navy in a Ukrainian excess defense article purchase initially offered in 2014.[79]

Georgia, which also lost the majority of its maritime and air capabilities during its 2008 conflict with Russia in South Ossetia, decided in 2009 to integrate its coast guard and navy into a border-policing role under the Ministry of Interior.[80] Overall, the combined force includes 21 patrol and coastal combatants, as well as one amphibious landing craft.[81] Georgia's air force operates three combat-capable aircraft.[82]

Turkey has the most significant overall naval capabilities of any Black Sea littoral state besides Russia, with 18 frigates, 53 patrol and coastal combatants (including six corvettes and 19 fast attack craft, 15 mine warfare and mine countermeasures vessels, and 12 hunter-killer submarines).[83] The Turkish navy also operates three naval aviation squadrons with antisubmarine warfare capabilities, and Turkey's air force includes 333 combat-capable aircraft.[84] These capabilities are stretched across the Black Sea, the Aegean, and the Mediterra-

---

[78] Jones, 2018.

[79] Illia Ponomarenko, "Ukraine Accepts Two US Patrol Boats After 4 Years of Bureaucratic Blockades," *Kyiv Post*, September 27, 2018.

[80] Kuimova and Wezeman, 2018a.

[81] "After Calls for Black Sea FONOPS," 2018; International Institute for Strategic Studies, 2018, p. 187.

[82] International Institute for Strategic Studies, 2018, p. 187.

[83] International Institute for Strategic Studies, 2018, p. 158.

[84] International Institute for Strategic Studies, 2018, pp. 158–159.

nean.[85] Although the total number of Turkish warships has remained generally steady over the past decade, the Turkish navy has benefited from a national military modernization program to strengthen Turkey's defense industry.[86] Between 2016 and 2018, the Turkish navy received six indigenously produced naval vessels, including two corvettes, a landing ship, two logistics supports ships, and a rescue ship.[87] Turkey has also launched a national frigate program—known as MILGEM, or "national ship"—that features I-class vessels able to carry longer-range weapons systems, as well as a program to develop a "light aircraft carrier" able to operate up to 12 F-35B jets and 12 helicopters.[88] Turkey's first indigenously-built assault carrier, The Andalou, is expected to be commissioned in the Turkish navy in 2020.[89] In the Black Sea context, Turkish analysts have claimed Turkish superiority in operational submarines, noting that they could theoretically prevent the Russian fleet from reaching the Turkish Straits during conflict.[90] The Turkish government discharged nearly half of its senior military leadership in the 2017 political purges, likely eroding the combat readiness of all of its forces, including the navy.[91]

---

[85] Four of the Turkish navy's 14 bases are on the Black Sea, with another three on the Sea of Marmara. Siemon T. Wezeman and Alexandra Kuimova, *Turkey and Black Sea Security*, SIPRI Background Paper, Solna, Sweden: Stockholm International Peace Research Institute, December 2018.

[86] Wezeman and Kuimova, 2018, table 2, p. 8.

[87] Burak Ege Bekdil, "Turkish Shipyards Join Forces to Develop First Locally Made Ship Engine," *Defense News*, April 16, 2018.

[88] Bekdil, 2018.

[89] H. I. Sutton, "Turkey's New Assault Carrier Will Transform Navy," *Forbes*, May 13, 2020.

[90] Kucera, 2016b.

[91] Carlotta Gall, "President Recep Tayyip Erdogan of Turkey Replaces Top Military Chiefs," *New York Times*, August 2, 2017.

CHAPTER THREE

Diverse Perspectives and Avenues for Russian Influence

Beyond military power, Russia maintains robust political and economic ties across the Black Sea region that could potentially be applied as levers of persuasion or coercion to influence the decisionmaking of littoral governments. In this region and others, Moscow has typically preferred to pursue nonmilitary tactics to achieve its objectives where feasible, given the relatively lower associated risks and costs. Russian military leaders have also observed the value in using nonmilitary means to prepare the political "battlefield" for military conflict if necessary.[1] In his oft-cited 2013 description of a world defined by increasingly complex political conflict, General Valery Gerasimov stated,

> The focus of applied methods of conflict has altered in the direction of the broad use of political, economic, informational, humanitarian, and other non-military measures—applied in coordination with the protest potential of the population. All this is supplemented by military means of a concealed character, including carrying out actions of informational conflict and the actions of special-operations forces. The open use of forces—often under the guise of peacekeeping and crisis regulation—is resorted to only at a certain stage, primarily for the achievement of final success in the conflict.[2]

---

[1] Mark Galeotti, *Russian Political War: Moving Beyond the Hybrid*, London: Routledge, 2019.

[2] V. P. Gulin, "O novoi kontseptsii voiny," *Voennaya mysl'*, Vol. 6, No. 3, 1997, cited in Galeotti, 2019, p. 18.

As it seeks to assert regional dominance, Russia has pursued a wide range of nonmilitary measures, including but not limited to tactics such as the dissemination of Kremlin-directed narratives by government media platforms and troll farms, cyber espionage and attacks, and the employment of irregular forces and criminals.[3] Previous works have also examined the Russian government's personal and financial relationships with political figures, investment in regional media markets, emerging energy projects and opportunities, trade dependencies, and popular cultural ties, all of which could affect the foreign policy calculations of national leaders in the region.[4]

Some have argued that Russia's 2012 intervention in Ukraine ultimately undermined its capacity for Black Sea political influence. In an article written in the months following Russia's 2014 intervention on the Crimean Peninsula, Black Sea naval scholar Deborah Sanders identified ways in which Russian military power was increasing in the region but observed that "it is important to understand that maritime power is about more than just capability: it is about influence."[5] U.S., NATO, and regional reactions to the Russian land grab, Sanders argued, had made the context of Russian power more problematic and thus made it more difficult for Russia to wield influence.[6]

Across the Black Sea region, wide-ranging divergences in regional perspectives on Russia could complicate consensus on any Western-led multilateral military response to Russian posturing. During a confrontation, precedent suggests that Russia would actively seek to sway the

---

[3]   Galeotti, 2019.

[4]   Most prominent among these is Bechev, 2017. A 2017 RAND publication examines key sources of European vulnerability to Russian influence—including military, energy, and political measures—and considers how they might translate into influence over policymaking. See F. Stephen Larrabee et al., *Russia and the West After the Ukrainian Crisis: European Vulnerabilities to Russian Pressures*, Santa Monica, Calif.: RAND Corporation, RR-1305-A, 2017.

[5]   Sanders, 2014. See also Deborah Sanders's 2016 assessment of Black Sea maritime power, in which she focuses predominantly on the military dimension of power but similarly concludes that "context" also affects the power to influence decisions, observing that "poor or strained relations with neighbors, or conversely good relations with neighbours, affect, at times, both directly and indirectly, the maritime power of all six littoral states." Deborah Sanders, *Maritime Power in the Black Sea*, London: Routledge, 2016, p. 191.

[6]   Sanders, 2014.

positions of regional governments in its favor. RAND's 2018 Black Sea game explored the extent to which Russia would be able to assert influence and power in order to impede a regional course of action that it opposed. The game sought to highlight critical considerations that could affect the positions of regional governments, and to consider how Russia might seek to exploit these issue areas during a crisis. The following sections provide a brief overview of considerations for regional decisionmakers in NATO's five Black Sea littoral partners and allies during a crisis with Russia, and whether and how these might translate into areas of Russian leverage.

Turkey

Turkey would prove a pivotal player in any Black Sea initiative because of its maritime capabilities, as well as its responsibility for controlling naval passage through the Turkish Straits from the Mediterranean to the Black Sea under the Montreux Convention. Turkey's regional position has been described as a "multi-vector approach" as Ankara seeks to balance its relationship with the United States with that of Russia.[7] Turkey's regional hedging strategy has contributed to cautious diplomatic responses to previous Russian land incursions in the Black Sea littoral states of Georgia in 2008 and Ukraine in 2014.[8]

Ankara has previously opposed U.S. initiatives that would extend NATO operations to the Black Sea.[9] In May 2015, Turkish navy

---

[7] Dmitar Bechev, "Turkey and Black Sea Security: Ten Years After the War in Georgia," *New Atlanticist* (Atlantic Council blog), August 8, 2018.

[8] In 2009, the Turks actively sought a balancing diplomacy with the Caucasus Stability and Cooperation Platform, which the Russians, the Georgians, and others in the region spurned. In 2014, Erdoğan called Russia's intervention in Crimea illegal and expressed concerns about the Crimean Tartars but was otherwise muted. See Soner Cagaptay and James F. Jeffrey, "Turkey's Muted Reaction to the Crimean Crisis," *Washington Institute*, March 4, 2014.

[9] Delanoe, 2014, p. 378. Delanoe notes that "when Washington suggested in 2006 to extend NATO Operation Active Endeavour to the Black Sea, both Moscow and Ankara strongly opposed. Whereas the former argued that littoral states were fully able to enforce maritime security on the Black Sea stage, the latter raised serious concerns about the implementation of the Montreux Convention in the context of increasing naval activity."

commander Admiral Bülent Bostanoğlu noted that although Russian actions in Ukraine had negatively affected Black Sea cooperation, Turkey maintained its policy that regional initiatives and mutual trust among the littoral Black Sea states should preserve maritime security in the Black Sea, highlighting Turkey's support for initiatives such as the Black Sea Naval Cooperation Task Group and Operation Black Sea Harmony.[10] Historically, Russia and Turkey have cooperated on regional initiatives, including the Black Sea Economic Council, which the United States was invited to join only at the insistence of other Black Sea states in the absence of Turkish support.[11] Turkey and Russia participate in joint military maritime drills in the Black Sea, even following Russia's military attacks on Ukraine.[12]

However, Ankara has at times supported an enhanced Western presence in the Black Sea, particularly during moments of bilateral tension with Russia. Historically, the 1946 port visit of the USS *Missouri*, ostensibly to deliver the ashes of the deceased Turkish ambassador to the United States, represented a tangible demonstration of emerging U.S. security guarantees in response to muscular Soviet efforts to coerce Turkey into yielding basing rights in the Dardanelle Straits.[13] More recently, President Recep Tayyip Erdoğan did call for a greater NATO presence in the Black Sea during the 2015–2016 Russia-Turkey diplomatic crisis, warning NATO's secretary general that the Black Sea was in danger of becoming a "Russian lake."[14] Turkey was also initially supportive of Romania's 2016 proposal—floated during Turkey's diplomatic rupture with Russia—for a NATO Black Sea Fleet.[15] At NATO's 2018 Brussels Summit, Ankara advocated for the extension

---

[10] "Admiral Bülent Bostanoglu, Commander, Turkish Navy," *Jane's Defence Weekly*, May 27, 2015.

[11] Fiona Hill and Omer Taspinar, "Turkey and Russia: The Axis of the Excluded?" *Survival*, Vol. 48, No. 1, 2006, pp. 81–92.

[12] Dave Majumdar, "Why Are Russia and Turkey Holding Joint Naval Exercises in the Black Sea?" *National Interest*, April 5, 2017.

[13] Reva Bhalla, "Turkey's Time Has Come," *Real Clear World*, December 10, 2015.

[14] "Erdogan Warns NATO Black Sea Has Become 'Russian Lake,'" *B92*, May 12, 2016.

[15] "Bulgaria Says Will Not Join," 2016.

of membership to Georgia, a policy that Moscow has consistently and forcefully opposed.[16]

Russia maintains several areas of influence on Turkish interests that it could potentially apply in an effort to shape Turkish positions in the region. In particular, Turkish interests in Syria, Russian energy ties, trade and tourism relations, and Russia's appeal as an alternative to NATO, the European Union, and the United States could all make Turkey wary of contributing to a rupture in relations.

Among these factors, Russia's role in Syria has the potential to provide the most significant source of leverage. Turkey's primary national security objective remains the defeat of the Kurdistan Workers' Party, and Turkey has pursued military operations to prevent a unified Kurdish region from emerging in Syria.[17] Russia's central role in determining the Syrian endgame as well as its historical willingness to support the Kurds in the face of objections from Ankara, may motivate Turkish leadership to seek to maintain a positive relationship with Russia. Turkey is likely to seek to maintain coordination with Russia in Syria in order to ensure Turkey's ability to "to clear [the region] of terror organizations such as the PYD [Democratic Union Party] and the YPG [People's Protection Units]" and ultimately to prevent the emergence of an independent Kurdish corridor.[18] However, while Russia's role in Syria and its relationship with the Kurds could afford it potential leverage, an overly coercive approach to the Kurdish question could potentially backfire, prompting another rupture in relations with Turkey and a greater willingness of Turkey to support an enhanced Western presence in the Black Sea.

Turkey's energy ties to Russia could provide additional sources of influence: Turkey relied on Russian gas for 56 percent of its total natural gas supply in 2015, as well as 11 percent of crude oil imports.[19] The

---

[16] Bechev, 2018.

[17] Amanda Sloat, "Turkey Wants to Crush U.S. Allies in Syria. That Shouldn't Surprise Anyone," *Order from Chaos* (Brookings Institution blog), January 24, 2018.

[18] Associated Press, "Russia, Turkey Mull Next Steps in War-Torn Syria," *Voice of America*, January 23, 2019.

[19] U.S. Energy Information Administration, *Country Analysis Brief: Turkey*, Washington, D.C., February 2, 2017.

completion of Gazprom's TurkStream gas pipeline, which can supply up to 1.1 trillion cubic feet of gas to Turkish—and eventually other European—markets is likely to further increase Turkish demand for Russian gas and fuel Turkey's broader ambitions to serve as a geostrategic energy hub.[20] Ultimately, TurkStream is likely to provide Russia with opportunities for additional economic incentives—what one author dubbed "petro-carrots"—that may make Turkey less willing to risk a rupture in relations.[21] The Turkish government has already explicitly politicized the issue of Russian gas prices during presidential bilateral engagements, and as of April 2019, Russia was reportedly considered giving Turkey a 10-percent gas price reduction.[22] Figure 3.1 identifies Turkish regional national gas pipelines and projects.

If an incentive-based approach failed, "petro-carrots" in the form of subsidized energy could theoretically transform into "petro-sticks."[23] However, coercive leverage offered by TurkStream would be mitigated by energy diversity provided by the Trans-Anatolian Natural Gas Pipeline project.[24] Turkey's investments to increase the capacity of its liquefied natural gas, build new terminals, and expand gas storage capacity would further reduce Russian gas leverage during a crisis.[25] In January 2019, liquefied natural gas made up more than 40 percent of total Turkish gas imports, while gas imports from

[20] Nik Martin, "TurkStream: Who Profits, Who Loses Out?" *Die Welt*, November 19, 2018. See also Dimitar Bechev, "Russia's Pipe Dreams Are Europe's Nightmare," *Foreign Policy*, March 12, 2019.

[21] Randall Newnham, "Oil, Carrots, and Sticks: Russia's Energy Resources as a Foreign Policy Tool," *Journal of Eurasian Studies*, Vol. 2, No. 2, 2011, pp. 134–143.

[22] "Russia May Give Turkey 10 Percent Gas Price Reduction—Report," *Ahval*, April 10, 2019; "Erdogan May Have Politicized Issue of Russian Gas Prices to Send a Signal to US—Expert," TASS, April 10, 2019.

[23] Newnham, 2011.

[24] "Turkey Opens TANAP Pipeline That Will Bring Azeri Gas to Europe," *Die Welt*, June 12, 2018.

[25] Gulmira Rzayeva, *Gas Supply Changes in Turkey*, Oxford: Oxford Institute for Energy Studies, January 2018.

Figure 3.1
Turkey's Regional Natural Gas Pipelines and Projects (Turkish Government)

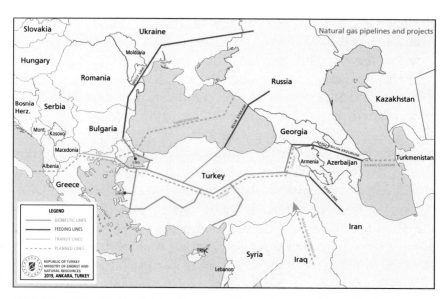

SOURCE: Republic of Turkey Ministry of Energy and Natural Resources, "Natural Gas Pipelines and Projects," 2019.
NOTE: The TANAP pipeline was completed in November 2019, and the Trans-Caspian Pipeline (TAP) is slated to be completed in 2020 ("Turkey and Azerbaijan Mark Completion of TANAP Pipeline to Take Gas to Europe," *Reuters*, November 30, 2019).

Russia decreased.[26] Additionally, any effort by Russia to use energy as a coercive tool against Turkey would have a detrimental effect on Russian energy markets.

Bilateral economic ties in the areas of tourism, construction, and agriculture represent another potential source of influence. Russia sought to apply coercive pressure to influence the Turkish government during 2015 Turkey-Russia shootdown crisis when it embargoed Turkish agricultural imports, restricted Russian tourism to Turkey, ended visa-free travel for Turkish citizens, and halted plans for the Turk-Stream gas pipeline.[27] At the time, Turkish economists predicted that

---

[26] "Turkey Hits Historic LNG Import Record in Jan," *Hurriyet Daily News*, March 30, 2019.

[27] "Russia Places Sanctions on Turkey," *New York Times*, November 29, 2015.

the short-term losses for the Turkish economy could eventually total as much as $10 billion.[28] Analysts noted that these could harm Russian economic interests as well.[29] Erdoğan ultimately did issue an apology, likely prompted by the prospect for cooperation with Russia in Syria, as well as the economic costs of Russian sanctions.[30]

Finally, Turkey's strained relationship with Western allies—including the United States—could further complicate the picture for Turkey, as Russia actively seeks to present an alternative model to the liberal Western order. The increasingly authoritarian Turkish government has repeatedly communicated frustration with European and U.S. leaders for their pressure on President Erdoğan's antidemocratic practices. Turkey's decision to purchase Russian S-400 air defense systems and retaliatory moves by the United States have further exacerbated tensions. Ultimately, differences between Turkey's bilateral relationships with Russia and the United States may put Russia at an advantage; while issues in the Russia-Turkey relationship are often compartmentalized, those in the U.S.-Turkey relationship crosscut a variety of issue areas that could hinder cooperation on a discrete Black Sea initiative. Active Russian campaigns to spread disinformation and perpetuate anti-U.S. conspiracy theories—including widely accepted claims in Russian-sponsored media that the United States sponsored the July 2016 coup attempt—could drive further wedges between Turkey and the United States and complicate any U.S.-led initiative in the Black Sea region.[31]

Romania

Romania has been the most vocal NATO ally to call for enhanced presence and activity in the Black Sea region. In 2008, following Rus-

---

[28] Selin Gerit, "Turkey Faces Big Losses as Russia Sanctions Bite," *BBC*, January 6, 2016.

[29] "Russia and Turkey Will Both Lose from Moscow's Sanctions," *CNN*, November 30, 2015.

[30] Jeffrey Mankoff, "A Friend in Need? Russia and Turkey After the Coup," *Center for Strategic and International Studies*, July 29, 2016.

[31] For additional background on the Russian application of disinformation in the Turkish media, see Katherine Costello, *Russia's Use of Media and Information Operations in Turkey: Implications for the United States*, Santa Monica, Calif.: RAND Corporation, PE-278-A, 2018.

sian military operations in Georgia, the Romanian government pressed NATO—as well as the United States—to prioritize the Black Sea.[32] As noted previously, the Romanian government actively pursued permanent rotations of NATO naval vessels in the Black Sea before the 2016 Warsaw Summit.

Moscow has no significant allies across the Romanian political spectrum, and in light of broad popular skepticism about Russian motives within the Romanian public, pro-Russian information operations have not yielded significant success.[33] However, Russian media sources have sought to perpetuate narratives that exacerbate social divisions or governance challenges, which could undermine government cohesion during a crisis.[34] Corruption, justice system reform, and taxes on Black Sea energy extraction remain divisive political debates that could potentially be exploited in an effort to destabilize Romania's leadership.[35] Similarly, narratives that reduce public trust in the NATO alliance—playing on potential concerns about NATO's lack of action, cohesion, and political will—could fuel doubts about military initiatives that could raise the ire of Russia.[36] Although Romanian intelligence services actively seek to thwart Russian intelligence activities on Romanian soil, lingering influence from Cold War KGB relationships reportedly remains.[37]

---

[32] Joja, 2018.

[33] "Executive Summary," in Oana Popescu and Rufin Zamfir, eds., *Propaganda Made-to-Measure: How Our Vulnerabilities Facilitate Russian Influence*, Bucharest: Global Focus Asymetric Threats Programme, February 2018, p. 14; Raphael S. Cohen and Andrew Radin, *Russia's Hostile Measures of Influence: Threats in Eastern Europe*, Santa Monica, Calif.: RAND, PR-2564/3A, October 2016, p. 89.

[34] "Executive Summary," 2018, p. 14; Cohen and Radin, 2016, p. 89.

[35] See Anca Gurzu, "Romania's Black Sea Gas Sparks Political Crisis," *Politico*, August 23, 2018.

[36] Corina Rebegea, "Living the Russian Dream," brief, *Center for European Policy Analysis*, July 19, 2017.

[37] Kremlin Watch Team, *Kremlin Influence in the Visegrad Countries and Romania*, Kremlin Watch memo, European Values Think-Tank and Wilfried Martens Centre for European Studies, October 23, 2017, p. 32.

Romania's domestic production of natural gas has shielded Bucharest from some of the economic manipulation that decisionmakers in Ankara and Sofia might need to consider. With only about 10 percent of Romanian gas imported from Russia, Romanian energy markets enjoy a degree of energy independence.[38] Further Romanian offshore Black Sea oil and gas extraction would provide an additional supply to Romanian and other regional markets, although Romania's regulatory environment has previously given some investors pause.[39] When Russia cut some 2014 gas deliveries to Romania without explanation—a move believed to have been in retaliation for Romanian support for Western sanctions against Russia—the Romanian government was relatively unconcerned.[40]

Because the Romanian government would be unlikely to change its position on the enhancement of NATO's Black Sea presence through an incentives-based approach, the Russian government could seek to leverage fear within the Romanian population and government to alter Romanian decisionmaking.[41] Romanian political leaders have consistently viewed Russia as a threat to Romanian security, economic, and political interests, and they remain particularly concerned about Russian activities in Moldova and in the Black Sea region.[42] The government position reflects the majority of Romanian public opinion: one 2016 poll found that 57 percent of Romanians identified Russia as the country posing the greatest threat to Romania.[43]

---

[38] "Romania Says Its Natural Gas Output Set to Double by 2025," Reuters, February 20, 2018.

[39] "Black Sea Oil & Gas to Go Ahead with $400 Million Romanian Offshore Project," Reuters, February 6, 2019.

[40] Romanian energy minister Răzvan Nicolescu stated at the time that "the decision is surprising, but we can deal with the situation. The population will not be affected even [if] gas deliveries from Russia are stopped completely." Marian Chiriac, "Romania Defiant over Russian Gas Squeeze," *Balkan Insight*, September 16, 2014.

[41] Rebegea, 2017.

[42] Kremlin Watch Team, 2017, p. 32.

[43] Neli Esipova and Julie Ray, "Eastern Europeans, CIS Residents See Russia, U.S. as Threats," *Gallup*, April 4, 2016.

Russian officials have already included military threats against Romania in their public statements. In 2014, Russian deputy prime minister Dmitry Rogozin threatened to return to Romania on a TU-160 strategic bomber after his plane was denied access to Romanian airspace.[44] In 2016, President Putin warned that Romania (as well as Poland) could find itself in Russian "crosshairs" as a result of their decision to host U.S. missile defense infrastructure.[45] Beyond rhetoric, Russian Su-30 and Su-27 aircraft have repeatedly flown close to Romanian airspace, prompting NATO aircraft to scramble.[46] Romanian defense minister Mihai Fifor noted in June 2018 that there is not "a single day without a challenge" from Russia in Romanian airspace or territorial waters, as well as "interference in the political zone, interference with minorities . . . and economic war."[47]

As Russia further sought to influence Romanian decisionmaking through tactics beneath the threshold of military conflict, it could potentially seek to escalate cyber operations against Romanian public and private institutions. Romanian government and nongovernment entities have been struck by rootkit hacking attacks, phishing attacks, and election cyber interference believed to have been linked to the Russian government.[48] Romanian Black Sea energy initiatives—which, in conjunction with U.S. companies, could transport Romanian gas to

---

[44] "Romania Wants Russia to Explain Official's Threatening Remarks," *Radio Free Europe/Radio Liberty*, May 11, 2014.

[45] Denis Dyomkin, "Putin Says Romania, Poland, May Now Be in Russia's Cross-Hairs," Reuters, May 27, 2016.

[46] For example, "British Jets Scramble from Romania to Investigate Russian Fighter Jets," *Radio Free Europe/Radio Liberty*, August 22, 2018. In October 2018, Royal Canadian Air Force CF-188 Hornets intercepted a Russian SU-27 Flanker aircraft operating near Romanian airspace over the Black Sea. Royal Canadian Air Force, cited in Chris Thatcher, "RCAF Hornets Intercept Russian Su-27 Flanker," October 26, 2018.

[47] Quoted in Associated Press, "Romania Minister Says Country Facing Cyber-Attacks, Russian," *Voice of America*, June 25, 2018.

[48] Robert Johnston, "Russia Ramps Up Cyber Warfare as It Loses Economic Footing in Ukraine," *The Hill*, December 13, 2018; Georgiana Bender, "Cyber Attack on Romanian Institution Foiled by Intelligence Services," *Business Review*, May 12, 2017.

Europe and provide further diversity beyond Russian sources—could also prove a potential target for plausibly deniable Russian activities.

Russian presence and activity in the Moldovan breakaway republic of Transnistria could represent another area for coercive pressure. Romanian threat perceptions are to a large degree grounded in century-old tensions with Russia over the geopolitical orientation of Moldova and the status of Transnistria.[49] Movements to reunify with Moldova have periodically captured the imagination of the Romanian public—and parliament.[50] Romanian leaders have explicitly linked Romania's increase in defense spending to Russian aggression in Ukraine and the potential for further military activities in Transnistria.[51] Russian actions that destabilize Moldova—including through Russia's military presence in Transnistria—could have a destabilizing effect on Romania's political climate.

Bulgaria

In February 2019, Bulgarian prime minister Boyko Borissov reassured NATO's secretary general that "Bulgaria is not the Trojan horse of Russia in NATO" and indeed was "one of the most disciplined and loyal members of the Alliance."[52] Within the Black Sea region, Bulgaria has welcomed some cooperative efforts with NATO allies. In 2016, it offered to contribute up to 400 troops to NATO's emergent Multinational Framework Brigade in Romania.[53] Bulgaria regularly hosts allied

---

[49] *The Economist* writes, "To Romanians, Russia is a predator. It took an eastern province from them in 1812. Romania regained it in 1918 and lost it again to the Soviet Union in 1940–41." "The New Kids on the Block," *The Economist*, January 4, 2007

[50] "Romanian Parliament Says Would Back Reunification with Moldova," Reuters, March 27, 2018.

[51] Paul McLeary, "With Demands for More NATO Spending, Romania Steps Up," *The Cable, Foreign Policy*, May 3, 2017.

[52] Michael-Ross Fiorentino, "PM Borissov Assures NATO Bulgaria Is Not Russia's 'Trojan Horse,'" *Euronews*, February 3, 2019.

[53] Toucas, 2017.

Black Sea exercises and visits, including the annual international Breeze exercise, which includes units from Belgium, Bulgaria, France, Greece, Italy, Poland, Romania, Turkey, the United States, and NATO's Allied Maritime Command.[54] In 2018, Bulgaria hosted visits from Standing NATO Maritime Group Two in Varna as part of the group's Black Sea patrol.[55]

However, a number of factors could potentially serve to influence Bulgarian decisionmaking in Russia's favor during a regional standoff between Russia and the West. Bulgaria maintains what one regional scholar has characterized as a "cautious, risk-averse attitude" toward Russia, seeking to build stronger partnerships with NATO and the European Union without antagonizing Russia.[56] Additionally, ties between Bulgarian government officials and the Kremlin create channels of influence that may not be publicly observed and measured. Extensive Russian investment in the Bulgarian economy—including high levels of foreign direct investment and most recently through energy projects—adds to the potential leverage. Local media outlets sponsored by Russian state or para-state institutions spread propaganda and disinformation that promote economic opportunities with Russia while disparaging U.S. and European interventionism.[57] Finally, Bulgarian fear about Russian retaliation—compounded by distrust of NATO's will to defend Bulgaria—could prompt Bulgaria to oppose actions in the Black Sea that might invite Russian retaliation.

One resource that Moscow could leverage would be its strong ties to the Bulgarian government, including with Bulgarian president Rumen Radev, who has closely echoed the Kremlin's positions on regional crisis, including the 2018 Kerch Strait incident, which he blamed on Ukraine.[58] Bulgarian intelligence services reportedly retain

---

[54] "Bulgarian-Hosted Exercise Breeze 2018 Concludes," *Naval Today*, July 24, 2018.

[55] "NATO Groups in Black Sea Make Port Calls in Bulgaria," *Naval Today*, February 12, 2018.

[56] Dimitar Bechev, *Russia's Influence in Bulgaria*, Brussels: New Direction, May 12, 2015.

[57] Dimitar Bechev, "Bulgaria," in Popescu and Zamfir, 2018, p. 138.

[58] "Bulgarian President Radev Blames Ukraine for Kerch Straits Crisis," *Sofia Globe*, November 30, 2018.

close ties to Moscow from the Soviet period, providing Moscow influence over Bulgarian policy and political strategies.[59] Pervasive corruption provides opportunities for Russian leverage on government officials, through both direct financial patronage and the potential release of compromising material.[60] The pro-Russia Ataka party, in coalition with the ruling GERB (Citizens for European Development of Bulgaria) party, has reportedly received funding from the Russian embassy and has earned plaudits from the Russian Duma.[61] The Bulgarian Socialist Party, the second-largest party in the Bulgarian parliament, also maintains a pro-Russian stance and engages directly with Putin's United Russia Party: in June 2016, Bulgarian Socialist Party leader Kornelia Ninova called for the revocation of Russian sanctions during a United Russia congress.[62] Bulgarian internal political debates on how to respond to a nerve agent attack on a former Russian spy in London reflect the political divisions that could emerge in an escalating confrontation. Although the ruling GERB party supported the decision made by the United States and most European Union partners to expel Russian diplomats following the attack, Ataka and other nationalist coalition partners opposed expulsion, as did the opposition Socialists and President Radev.[63] Ultimately Sophia announced that it would not expel Russian diplomats, in the interest of maintaining dialogue with Moscow.[64]

---

[59] Larrabee et al., 2017. See also Joe Parkinson and Georgi Kantchev, "Document: Russia Uses Rigged Polls, Fake News to Sway Foreign Elections," *Wall Street Journal*, March 23, 2017.

[60] Bechev, "Bulgaria," in Popescu and Zamfir, 2018, p. 152.

[61] Jo Simmons, "The Curious Tale of Bulgaria's Extremist Flip-Flopping Party," *Huffington Post*, June 3, 2014.

[62] Heather Conley et al., *The Kremlin Playbook: Understanding Russian Influence in Central and Eastern Europe*, report of the Center for Strategic and International Studies Europe Program and the Center for the Study of Democracy Economics Program, Lanham, Md.: Rowman and Littlefield, October 2016, p. 43.

[63] Alissa de Carbonnel and Tsvetelia Tsolova, "Old Ties with Russia Weigh on Bulgarian Decision in Spy Poisoning Case," Reuters, March 29, 2018.

[64] "Bulgaria Says Will Not Expel Russian Diplomats over Spy Poisoning," Reuters, March 30, 2018.

Energy considerations also have the potential to influence Bulgarian decisionmaking. Bulgaria is almost entirely dependent on Russian gas, via Gazprom, for its national energy consumption.[65] Russian crude oil continues to form 84 percent of Bulgaria's total oil consumption.[66] Furthermore, Lukoil Group represents the Bulgarian government's largest taxpayer—making up about one-quarter of all national budget revenues in the country—and makes up about 9 percent of Bulgaria's overall gross domestic product.[67] The potential influence created by Bulgaria's energy ties to Russia has been previously noted by Russian energy executives: in 2001, Lukoil's president commented that he was "certain that Bulgaria, whose oil sector is almost entirely owned by Russian companies, will not conduct an anti-Russian foreign policy in the foreseeable future."[68]

Although Bulgaria has been pursuing energy independence, current plans for the second phase of the TurkStream project to bring Russian gas directly to Bulgaria could reduce incentives to diversify and increase opportunity for Russian influence, particularly in light of Bulgaria's aspirations to become a regional gas hub and a potential Bulgarian investment of €1.4 billion ($1.6 billion) in the project.[69] Russian coercive pressure would be limited by the construction of a natural gas interconnector between Greece and Bulgaria, approved by the European Commission for public support in November 2018, which could help Bulgaria to diversify its gas.[70] Bulgaria has contract with Azerbaijan for 1 billion cubic meters of Azeri gas, which will become available

---

[65] "Bulgaria to Build New Link to Turkey in Hope of Russian Gas," Reuters, June 26, 2018.

[66] Bechev, 2017, p. 210.

[67] Conley et al., 2016, p. 46.

[68] Quoted in Fiona Hill, "Beyond Co-Dependency: European Reliance on Russian Energy," *Brookings Institution*, July 1, 2005.

[69] Peter Cholakov, "Russia's Proposed TurkStream 2 Pipeline Sparks Bulgaria, EU Energy Worries," *Die Welt*, February 28, 2019.

[70] European Commission, "State Aid: Commission Approves Public Support for Natural Gas Interconnector Between Greece and Bulgaria," press release, European Union, Brussels, November 8, 2018.

once the Trans-Anatolian Natural Gas Pipeline and Trans-Adriatic Pipeline are in place and the Greek interconnector is operational.[71]

Bulgarian financial ties with Russia might also be leveraged in an effort to influence decisionmaking. Of the countries in the Black Sea region, Bulgaria has the highest percentage of Russian foreign direct investment and portfolio investment flows, at between 5 and 11 percent of Bulgaria's national gross domestic product—a factor that, if leveraged by Russia, could have influence on policy positions in Sofia.[72] Bulgarian estimates of Russian investment in Bulgarian real estate exceed €1 billion.[73] Russian foreign direct investment has focused on strategic sectors beyond energy, including real estate and the media, potentially providing Russian investors with disproportionate influence in these areas.[74] Bulgaria is currently seeking funding to restart work on a nuclear power plant in Belene, Bulgaria: Russian prime minister Dmitry Medvedev has stated that the Russian nuclear energy firm Rosatom is ready to invest in the project, and Bulgarian officials report that the plant cannot be completed without Rosatom.[75] If Rosatom provides major funding for the Belene project, it could open additional avenues for Russian influence in Bulgaria.[76]

Ultimately, deep-seated Bulgarian concerns about Russian military and economic retaliation could provide Moscow with opportunities for a combination of incentives and potential coercion. Concerns

---

[71] Leman Mammadova, "Bulgaria Eyes to Receive Additional Gas from Azerbaijan," *Azernews*, March 15, 2019.

[72] Larrabee et al., 2017. The authors note that "if Russian investors began to move to sell these assets, the localized effect could erode these small economies' support for Western-imposed sanctions" (Larrabee et al., 2017, p. 27). See also Conley et al., 2016, p. 46.

[73] Bulgarian National Bank, cited in Paul Stronski and Annie Himes, *Russia's Game in the Balkans*, working paper, Washington, D.C.: Carnegie Endowment for International Peace, January 2019, p. 7.

[74] Conley et al., 2016, p. 46.

[75] "Bulgaria Seeks Funding for Second Nuclear Power Plant," *Radio Free Europe/Radio Liberty*, March 11, 2019.

[76] Bradley Hanlon and Alexander Roberds, "Securing Bulgaria's Future: Combating Russian Energy Influence in the Balkans," *Alliance for Securing Democracy*, June 21, 2018.

about Russia are in part a function of Bulgarian lack of confidence about NATO's—and particularly U.S.—commitments to collective security: only one-third of Bulgarians believe the United States would use force to defend Bulgaria in the event of a serious conflict with Russia.[77] Russian cyber attacks have directly targeted Bulgarian government institutions, in one case causing the shutdown of the Central Electoral Commission website in October 2015.[78] At the highest levels of the Bulgarian government, Prime Minister Borissov has publicly stated that "Bulgaria would not allow itself to be attacked by Russia," and he criticized Western allies for failing to support Bulgaria in the face of Russian threats following Sofia's decision not to support South Stream or build a nuclear reactor with Russian technology.[79]

Bulgaria has previously yielded to Russian concerns in the face of warnings from Moscow. Perhaps most notable for the purposes of the RAND game, the Bulgarian decision not to support Romania's proposal for a NATO Black Sea Fleet came a day after Moscow warned that any "decision . . . to create a permanent force [in the Black Sea] would be destabilizing, because this is not a NATO sea."[80] Although the Bulgarian government's stated desire to protect nonmilitary usage of the Black Sea was likely genuine, the economic, political, and military implications of a rupture in Bulgaria's relationship with Russia were no doubt a core consideration as well.

---

[77] Pew Research Center, "Views on Role of Russia in the Region, and the Soviet Union," chapter 7 in *Religious Belief and National Belonging in Central and Eastern Europe*, Washington, D.C., May 10, 2017.

[78] Georgi Gotev, "At EU Summit, Borissov Deplores 'Terrible' Russian Cyberattacks on Bulgaria," *Euractiv*, October 18, 2018.

[79] Prime Minister Borissov reportedly stated in 2016, "You remember how our nuclear reactors from the Belene central left for Turkey. Not a single colleague spoke in my defense when President Putin, in the presence of Erdogan, waived his finger at me, saying that Bulgaria lost everything." Georgi Gotev, "Bulgaria Refuses to Join NATO Black Sea Fleet Against Russia," *Euractiv*, June 16, 2016.

[80] "Bulgaria Says Will Not Join," 2016; "Russia Warns NATO Not to Build Up Naval Forces in Black Sea," Reuters, June 15, 2016.

Ukraine

Russia's military interventions in Crimea and eastern Ukraine since 2014 have had a negative impact on its ability to attract regional governments to its preferred policy outcomes.[81] Ukraine was perhaps the most striking example of this development. Local polling indicated that 69 percent of Ukrainians would join NATO in 2017 if offered the opportunity, a dramatic surge from 2012 polling data indicating public support of only 29 percent.[82] Since 2014, the current Ukrainian government has consistently advocated for a greater NATO and U.S. presence in Ukraine.[83] In 2017, the Ukrainian Rada included NATO membership as a national strategic goal.[84] After the November 2018 Kerch Strait incident, Ukrainian president Petro Poroshenko urged NATO to deploy U.S. Navy vessels to the Sea of Azov—a highly provocative action that the alliance declined to pursue.[85]

Some traditional sources of Russian nonmilitary influence in Ukraine have also eroded in recent years. Most notably, Ukrainian energy diversification since 2015 has significantly reduced Russia's ability to inflict punishment on Ukrainian energy supplies. As of 2013, Russian gas accounted for over half of Ukrainian gas consumption.[86] Since then, domestic production, reverse flows from European partners such as Slovakia, and a reduction in domestic gas consumption

---

[81] Ukraine's increasing turn toward the West and its impact on the "context" in which Russia wields influence is noted in Sanders, 2014.

[82] Pavel Polityuk and Natalia Zinets, "Pledging Reforms by 2020, Ukraine Seeks Route into NATO," Reuters, July 10, 2017; "Public Opinion of the Population of Ukraine on NATO," *Ilko Kucheriv Democratic Initiatives Foundation*, July 5, 2017.

[83] Ukraine seeks a NATO Membership Action Plan by "no later than 2023," according to President Petro Poroshenko. "Ukraine President Signs Constitutional Amendment on NATO, EU Membership," *Radio Free Europe/Radio Liberty*, February 19, 2019.

[84] International Institute for Strategic Studies, *The Military Balance 2019*, London: Routledge for the International Institute for Strategic Studies, 2019, p. 212.

[85] Yuras Karamanau and Vladimir Isachenkov, "Ukraine Urges NATO to Deploy Ships in Dispute with Russia," Associated Press, November 29, 2018.

[86] Anton Antonekno et al., "Reforming Ukraine's Energy Sector: Critical Unfinished Business," *Carnegie Europe, Reforming Ukraine Project*, February 6, 2018.

have allowed Ukraine to end Russian gas imports entirely.[87] Ukraine's economy has also restored stability more broadly in the wake of the 2014 Russian military intervention.[88]

However, other Ukrainian economic and military vulnerabilities continue to offer Russia coercive levers of influence. Ukraine's dependence on maritime trade routes makes Russian assertion of power in the Black Sea particularly problematic for the Ukrainian economy. The Ukrainian Ministry of Infrastructure estimates that total financial losses from Russian shipping limitations in the Kerch Strait stand at US$20–$40 million annually.[89] Although Ukraine lost five ports located in Crimea during Russia's 2014 intervention, four important commercial ports in Odessa, Chornomorsk, Yuzhny, and Mariupol in the Sea of Azov remain and account for almost 70 percent of the total commercial cargo into Ukraine.[90] Thus Russia's increasingly assertive stance in the Sea of Azov has had economic as well as military ramifications for Ukraine.

Ongoing Russian involvement in Ukraine's eastern regions presents another potential vulnerability. Threats by Moscow (or separatist proxies) to expand the ground conflict in eastern Ukraine beyond its current front lines could certainly apply new pressures to the Ukrainian government. However, significant ground escalation would entail significant diplomatic, military, and economic costs to Russia—as one analyst has noted, "Such operations will only likely prolong the war and heighten the costs to Moscow and arouse even stronger NATO

---

[87] Ukrainian gas consumption also dropped by nearly 40 percent between 2013 and 2016, from 50.4 billion cubic meters in 2013 to 33.3 billion cubic meters in 2016, as a result of economic constriction, as well as the loss of energy-intensive industrial facilities in eastern Ukraine. Antonekno et al., 2018; Tim Daiss, "Ukraine Celebration: One Year Without Russian Gas," *Forbes*, November 27, 2016.

[88] David Clark, "Ukraine's Economy Has Turned a Corner," *Financial Times*, July 4, 2017.

[89] Krzysztof Nieczypor, "A Closely Watched Basin: The Russian–Ukrainian Tensions in the Sea of Azov," *Centre for Eastern Studies*, August 8, 2018.

[90] Sanders, 2017.

resistance at a time when Moscow has shown no desire to widen the scope of its kinetic combat operations against Ukraine."[91]

Georgia

Since the 2003 election of its first pro-Western government, Georgia has consistently advocated for an enhanced U.S. and NATO presence in the Black Sea region. Russia's 2008 intervention in Georgia—likely prompted in part by NATO's 2008 statement that Georgia (and Ukraine) would one day become a member of NATO—reinforced that position.[92] The Georgian government reiterated its readiness to support an enhanced NATO Black Sea presence at 2017 NATO Parliamentary Assembly meetings in Tbilisi.[93] Georgia has maintained its official position despite 2018 warnings from Moscow of a "terrible conflict" should Georgia seek to join NATO.[94]

Russia has previously applied a range of economic, military, and political levers of power to seek to undermine Georgian decisionmaking. In the years following the 2003 election and subsequent protests that ousted Communist leader Eduard Shevardnadze in favor of pro-Western candidate Mikheil Saakashvili, Russian suppliers increased Georgia's gas prices nearly fivefold.[95] Paired with punitive economic measures against the Western-leaning Saakashvili government—including 2006 sanctions on Georgian wine and produce and the expulsion of Georgian guest workers—these measures contributed to a

---

[91] Stephen Blank, "How the US Can Shore Up Ukraine's Vulnerabilities in the Black Sea," *UkraineAlert* (Atlantic Council blog), March 21, 2018.

[92] In 2011 then-President Medvedev stated of the Georgia conflict in a speech to soldiers, "If you . . . had faltered back in 2008, the geopolitical situation would be different now . . . and a number of countries which [NATO] tried to deliberately drag into the alliance, would have most likely already been part of it now." Quoted in Denis Dyomkin, "Russia Says Georgia War Stopped NATO Expansion," Reuters, November 21, 2011.

[93] Kuimova and Wezeman, 2018a.

[94] "Shrinking the Black Sea," *The Economist*, February 16, 2019.

[95] Newnham, 2011.

weak economy and resultant political challenges.[96] A "passportization" campaign to grant Russian passports to ethnic Russians and Russian speakers in breakaway Georgian republics created a pretext for Russian intervention in support of new citizens in the run-up to the 2008 conflict and continues today.[97] Ultimately, Russian proxy operations in South Ossetia, Georgian responses, and the subsequent 2008 military conflict between Russia and Georgia further eroded public and international support for the Saakashvili government.

Since 2008, Georgia has taken steps to reduce its vulnerability to Russian coercion. After the 2006 Russian ban on Georgian wine and mineral waters, exporters found other international buyers and were able to achieve a limited rebound.[98] Russia's 2012 accession to the World Trade Organization provided the Georgian government with WTO-based tools to challenge Russian trade restrictions, and the ban was lifted in 2013.[99] After hackers—likely connected to the Russian government—shut down Georgian government servers before and during the 2008 military conflict, the Georgian government established the Data Exchange Agency with a computer emergency response team to identify and mitigate cyber attacks.[100] The Georgian government has sought alternative sources of gas—particularly from Azerbaijan—and announced in early 2018 that it would not import Russian gas.[101] Georgia has been a net exporter of electricity to Russia since 2007.[102]

---

[96] Newnham, 2011.

[97] Agnia Grigas, *Beyond Crimea: The New Russian Empire*, New Haven, Conn.: Yale University Press, 2016.

[98] Sergi Kapanadze, *Georgia's Vulnerability to Russian Pressure Points*, London: European Council on Foreign Relations, June 2014.

[99] Kapanadze, 2014.

[100] Irakli Lomidze, "Cyber Attacks Against Georgia," briefing slides, Tbilisi, Georgia: Ministry of Justice of Georgia, Data Exchange Agency, 2011.

[101] Thea Morrison, "Georgia Not to Purchase Gas from Russia in 2018," *Georgia Today*, January 9, 2018.

[102] Kapanadze, 2014.

Despite these steps, Georgia remains vulnerable to Russian coercive pressures. One area Russia might explore would be remittances from Georgians living in Russia. According to the World Bank, Georgia received nearly 12 percent of its gross domestic product from remittances in 2017, of which Russia is the largest source.[103] However, as one analyst has noted, a Russian decision to end remittances would negatively affect Russian credibility and requires practical challenges to implement.[104]

Russia could also seek to undermine Georgian security through military and intelligence activities. Russia has placed as many as 4,000 military and security force personnel in each of Georgia's breakaway regions of Abkhazia and South Ossetia, and it could leverage this presence in an effort to destabilize the Georgian government. One current activity has included arbitrary detentions by Russian intelligence services of Georgian civilians for up to several months for so-called illegal border crossings along occupation lines.[105] Massing conventional forces could also assert pressure: before Russia's 2008 intervention in Georgia, Russia conducted large-scale military exercises near the Georgian border to practice scenarios including the defense of Russian "peacekeepers" and "citizens" in Abkhazia and South Ossetia against attack.[106] Ultimately, a Russian annexation attempt in either of the regions—or a successful campaign to gain international recognition for the regions—would prove deeply problematic for the Georgian government.[107]

---

[103] "Personal Remittances Received—Georgia," *World Bank Group*, 2019. In 2017, remittances from Russia represented 32.5 percent of total remittances, ahead of Italy and Greece. "Russia: Georgia's Largest Source of Remittances," *Georgia Today*, January 20, 2018.

[104] Kapanadze, 2014.

[105] Georgian Ministry of Foreign Affairs, *Quarterly Report on Human Rights Abuses in the Occupied Territories*, January 2016.

[106] Jim Nichol, *Russia-Georgia Conflict in August 2008: Context and Implications for U.S. Interests*, Washington, D.C.: Congressional Research Service, CRS Report RL34618, March 3, 2009.

[107] Kapanadze, 2014.

CHAPTER FOUR

Tailored Russian Tactics, Constrained Regional Responses

A June 2018 game designed by RAND sought to explore how Russian military and nonmilitary instruments of power in the Black Sea region might be brought to bear to pursue Russian interests during a limited military competition with Western powers. Specifically, the game sought to consider what measures Russia might employ to hinder efforts by NATO allies and partners to enhance defense and deterrence in the Black Sea region, and how Russian activities might constrain Western options. The game was staffed by researchers and policy practitioners with deep expertise in the region—generally players had studied the nations they were representing over their professional careers; in some cases the researchers were recruited from the nation being simulated. Ultimately, participants representing Russia were able to exploit preexisting divisions among NATO allies and partners in the region in order to erode unity around—but not entirely preclude—a coherent regional defense and deterrence initiative.

The game featured three stages. In the first stage, players were divided into teams representing the United States, Russia, and seven regional nations—the five Black Sea littoral states plus Moldova, which has access to the Black Sea through the river port of Giurgiulesti, and Greece, which controls the Souda Bay. The teams conducted a strategic assessment of their national interests in a projected political-military crisis scenario. Teams also identified potential actions available to turn the situation in their favor. In the last two stages, players charted out a potential series of responses as the crisis played out.

In each stage, the U.S. team proposed a multilateral response and made specific demands of each country to contribute political and military support to the effort. The Russia team was then able to use a wide range of political, military, and economic levers against each Black Sea country (or all of NATO), each of which was written on a card that could be presented to the relevant team to represent the action being taken. The seven regional teams then responded to both U.S. demands and Russian pressure by playing cards, again each representing a political-military action available to the nation. While the RAND team generated initial U.S. demands and cards for Russia and the Black Sea states, all players could add new actions simply by creating a new card.

A Black Sea Scenario

To consider how Russia might seek to influence regional decision-making during a military competition, RAND developed a scenario that extrapolated from current Russian activities and statements to elicit a crisis. The scenario—set sometime between 2020 and 2025—posited that Russia, concerned about strengthening military ties between Romania and Moldova and about an enhanced NATO maritime presence in the Black Sea, responded with a more aggressive maritime posture in the Black Sea that included warnings against foreign military activities in Russia's expanded EEZ claims, harassment of workers on offshore Romanian oil rigs, and intensification of information and cyber operations within Romania. The EEZ identified by the scenario's Russia reflected Russian post-2014 claims, which touch on the Romanian and Bulgarian EEZs, as indicated in Figure 4.1.[1]

---

[1]   William J. Broad, "In Taking Crimea, Putin Gains a Sea of Fuel Reserves," *New York Times*, May 17, 2014. The scenario element was derived from similar Chinese statements in the South China Sea. Maritime strategy scholar James Holmes later compared Russia's 2018 actions in the Sea of Azov to Chinese efforts to assert ownership in the South China Sea, a strategy that might later be applied elsewhere in the Black Sea. See Andrew Higgens, "Russia Slowly Throttles a Ukrainian Port," *New York Times*, December 14, 2018.

Figure 4.1
Russian Exclusive Economic Zones Claims Following Crimea Intervention

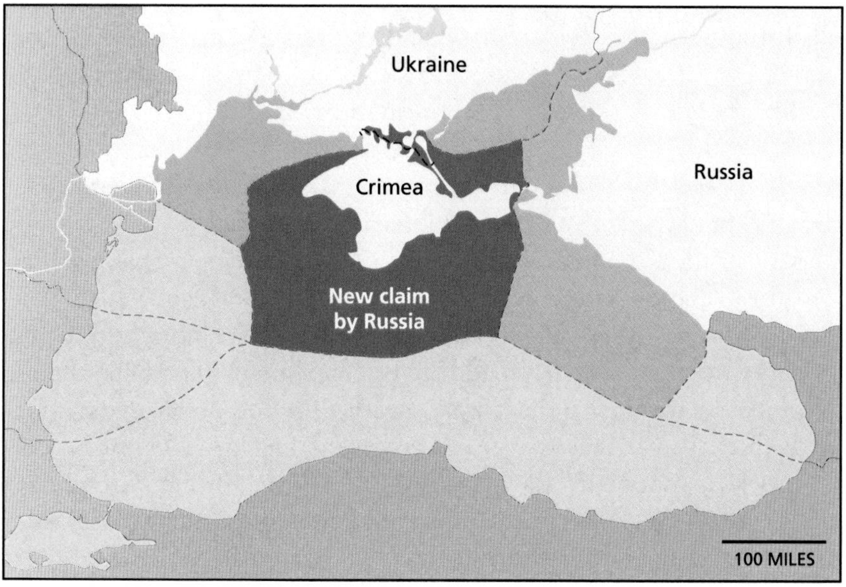

SOURCE: Adapted from Broad, 2014.

As exercising NATO vessels entered the waters to assert the principle of freedom of navigation, Russian Su-24 fighter-bomber jets buzzed a U.S. destroyer. Manifesting ongoing concerns regarding the safety of such actions, one fictional jet ultimately flew too close, clipping the destroyer and killing U.S. sailors and other NATO naval liaison officers.[2]

---

[2] After several Russian aircraft repeatedly flew close to a U.S. destroyer in 2017, U.S. European Command warned that "incidents like this concern us because they could possibly result in accident or miscalculation." Corey Dickstein, "Pentagon: Russian Aircraft Flew Too Close to US Destroyer in Black Sea," *Stars and Stripes*, February 14, 2017. In November 2018, 17 Russian aircraft from Crimea buzzed a British destroyer operating as part of Standing NATO Mine Countermeasures Group Two. Christopher Woody, "'Good Luck, Guys': 17 Russian Jets Buzzed a British Destroyer and Left a Threatening Message Earlier This Year," *Business Insider*, November 27, 2018.

Identifying Military Decision Points

The United States, played by members of the RAND study team, identified military options that could enhance defense and deterrence activities in the region in order to structure regional decisionmaking within the game. These included both immediate activities and longer-term initiatives and incorporated input from the players of regional teams, as well as the internal expertise of RAND's project team.

In particular, the game explored the potential for a revival of a variant of the Romanian proposal of 2016 to develop a regional Black Sea Task Force—either NATO led or multilateral—in which Black Sea navies and other NATO allies and partners, including the United States, would participate. In addition to local maritime assets, the task force could include, for example, heel-to-toe rotational deployments of U.S. destroyers based in Rota (Forward Deployed Naval Force—Europe), components of Standing NATO Maritime Group Two or Standing NATO Mine Countermeasures Group Two, and additional UK and French warships (i.e., FS *Aquitaine* or a *Cassard*-class air defense frigate). Alternative headquarters locations were proposed by participants, including the port Odessa, the current host of Sea Breeze, as well as the Georgian port of Batumi. Box 4.1 identifies initial requests from the U.S. team.

From these initial proposals, the U.S. team identified specific contributions that individual governments could make to the initiative and posited these as requests in order to prompt decision points within each of the country teams. In most cases, these included diplomatic support for—and eventually contributions to—the notional Black Sea Task Force. The U.S. team also requested host nation support and infrastructure investments for expanded U.S. presence at Novo Selo (Bulgaria) and Mihail Kogalniceanu Air Base in Romania. Turkey was asked to provide political support and contributions to the task force, to provide access to Trabzon and Cigli Air Bases for expanded Poseidon antisubmarine aircraft, and to consider enforcing Montreux limitations on the return of Russian submarines from the Mediterranean to the Black Sea. All NATO allies and partners were asked to increase investment in naval and coast guard capabilities. Moldova was asked to host NATO special forces for training

Box 4.1
Initial Proposals from U.S. Team

Black Sea Task Force to enable freedom-of-navigation operations
- coalition regional participation through access, basing, logistics
- coalition regional contribution of naval vessels
- heel-to-toe deployments of U.S. Destroyers based in Rota (Forward Deployed Naval Force—Europe)
- components of Standing NATO Maritime Group Two or Standing NATO Mine Countermeasures Group Two

Improve intelligence, surveillance, and reconnaissance capability in Black Sea
- deploy antisubmarine warfare aircraft to Trabzon and Cigli airbases

Expand Sea Breeze and Sea Shield exercises
- coordinated air exercises
- amphibious landing scenarios on Black Sea littoral coasts
- additional antisubmarine elements

Enhanced NATO/U.S. presence in littoral states
- surge of multinational amphibious forces at Novo Selo
- increased Western air presence at Mihail Kogalniceanu Air Base

Restrict power projection of Russian warships going into Mediterranean
- Montreux restrictions on submarine transit
- apply Montreux Article 21 to restrict Russian warships; enforce limitations on Russian Black Sea Fleet submarines deployed in the Mediterranean

---

and exercises, as well as to pledge to undertake military and political reforms to meet NATO standards.

During country team discussions, a number of additional non-military courses of action were identified, including engagement with the European Union to consider economic and political response options. Although these options would certainly be present in a real-world scenario, the game design limited Western response options to the military realm in order to focus the scope of discussion and test more difficult national security decisions.

Application of Tailored Russian Tactics

While strategic assessment varied across different members of the Russian team, many identified the same several interests in the Black Sea as likely to be central to Russian calculations in response to the game scenario. These interests included

- countering challenges to national sovereignty, including in Crimea
- maintaining a strategic buffer against NATO to limit expansion of U.S./NATO influence and presence in the region
- enhancing influence in the Black Sea region and bringing Eurasian states back into the Russian sphere
- demonstrating Russia's role as a great power and avoiding appearing weak
- maintaining freedom of navigation of Black Sea
- maintaining energy exports.

The risk of most concern to all players on the Russia team was the potential for uncontrolled escalation, leading to conflict with NATO and the United States. One participant applied prospect theory to explain potential Russian acceptance of risk during a crisis scenario: Russia's risk tolerance in the Black Sea would likely depend on its perceptions of potential losses; it would seek to achieve its objectives at minimal cost, but it would escalate if it felt it was likely to experience significant losses in the region. Perceptions varied across the Russia team: several players viewed the scenario primarily in opportunistic terms, considering it to be "ripe with opportunities to consolidate Russian influence," while others viewed it through the prism of potential losses, highlighting the need to "maintain" pressure on NATO to prevent it from reversing Russian gains in the Black Sea region. Participants agreed that in a real-world scenario, Russia would likely employ a variety of gray-zone activities, including both nonmilitary incentives and coercive measures, in an effort to undermine regional cohesion before escalating to military measures.

This approach was evidenced in the cards Russia opted to play to restrain the response of the Black Sea states. Throughout the game, Russia players elected to focus predominantly on nonmilitary measures, particularly toward countries that appeared willing to be influenced by incentives. However, the Russia team did flex its regional military superiority in actions taken against the collective group of regional partners and allies, including tracking NATO vessels entering the

Black Sea with *Kilo*-class submarines and issuing verbal warnings that Russian Bastion coastal missile systems and cruise-missile-armed subs can target potential aggressors in their ports of embarkation 500 km away. As the scenario escalated, these threats were underscored by Russian decisions to move all regional Russian military forces to combat alert status, to announce the placement of Russian Iskander missiles in Crimea, to conduct missile exercises demonstrating Russia's ability to cut off broad swaths of the Black Sea, and to temporarily restrict sections of the sea to commercial ship traffic.

Although the Russia team did offer a number of energy incentives—particularly for Turkey and Bulgaria—it did not elect to use energy resources as a coercive tool. This may have reflected an understanding by the Russia team that the likely target countries—Romania, Ukraine, and Georgia—had sufficiently diversified their energy sources to mitigate the effects of this tactic.

The tactics employed by Russia players against individual countries in the Black Sea region were informed by their assessment of perceived vulnerabilities of the target states, as well as the likelihood that incentives would be successful in securing Russian interests. Box 4.2 presents examples of Russia team cards played against other country teams. In particular, Turkey's deepening ties with Russia made it difficult to envision robust Turkish support of a major military initiative that would threaten Turkish economic and defense interests. The Russia team therefore focused on a variety of incentives—including lowered gas prices through the TurkStream pipeline and offers of enhanced Syria-related intelligence and territorial pledges—to shore up Turkish opposition to any plan bolstering the NATO or U.S. presence in the Black Sea. Should these fail, Team Russia was prepared to levy food and tourism restrictions against Turkey and—if need be—to threaten closer coordination with the People's Protection Units in Syria.

The Russia team similarly pursued an incentive-based approach to Bulgaria. To further dissuade Team Bulgaria from supporting or participating in a Black Sea Task Force initiative, Russia players applied energy incentives and diplomatic outreach, including a presidential summit. Media operations blaming NATO and the United States for the crisis and outreach to pro-Russia elements of Bulgaria's ruling coalition sought to influence political and public discourse

Box 4.2
Sample Russia Team Cards

For Turkey team
- Propose additional joint Black Sea military exercises.
- Propose a bilateral presidential summit.
- Offer intelligence on the Democratic Union Party in Syria.

For Bulgaria team
- Propose a bilateral presidential summit.
- Communicate with Ataka to call for NATO de-escalation.
- Offer below-market gas via Giurgiu-Ruse interconnector; offer to fund Belene.
- Blame NATO and the United States for the crisis in Russian-supported media outlets.

For Romania team
- Engage in election interference and information warfare.
- Harass commercial vessels.

For Ukraine team
- Blockade a Ukrainian fishing fleet in the Azov Sea.

For Georgia team
- Engage in snap exercises in occupied Georgian territory.

surrounding Bulgarian decisionmaking. The Russia team also indicated plans to threaten the Bulgarian leadership directly with information that could damage its members' reputations if an incentives strategy was unsuccessful.

In contrast, Russia players predominantly pursued coercive pressures against Romania, Georgia, and Ukraine in light of all three countries' strong starting positions in favor of enhanced Western presence in the Black Sea. For Romania, these tactics included election interference, as well as harassment of Romanian commercial vessels. Russian military signaling—particularly the previously noted missile exercises over the Black Sea—were particularly intended to intimidate and deter the Romanian audience.

For NATO partners Georgia and Ukraine, which both took starting positions in favor of the task force initiative, the Russia team pursued a primarily coercive approach that was not constrained by concerns about allied collective defense commitments. For Georgia, tactics included a smear campaign against politicians in support of the task force, as well as actions targeting the business interests of Georgian political leaders. Once these measures proved unsuccessful, the Russia team conducted snap exercises in Georgia's breakaway republics and promoted unrest in the predominantly Armenian-populated Samtskhe-Javakheti, raising the possibility of a third separatist region.

For the Moldova team, which appeared on the fence but wary of the potential for Russian retaliation, the Russia team leaked information about alleged corruption within pro-Western parties, made a presidential public statement calling for Moldovan-Russian unity, and eventually offered a trade deal with the Eurasian Economic Union.

Figure 4.2 illustrates the extent to which the ratio of incentives to disincentives and the selected instruments of power varied among target countries, as well as the NATO alliance. The Russia team took an almost exclusively incentives-based and nonmilitary approach to Turkey and Bulgaria across both rounds. These two NATO allies, as well as Moldova, continued to receive additional incentives as it became clear that they were wavering in their support for the regional task force initiative. For the other countries in the region, the Russia team undertook an increasingly coercive militarized approach in the second round of the game as their nonmilitary tactics met with mixed success.

The Limited and Disparate Responses of the Black Sea Country Teams

Ultimately, the Russia team was partially successful in its efforts to disrupt regional cohesion around a military response. Although the game's Turkey offered tepid initial political support of the task force, it insisted that the initiative be moved to fall under NATO auspices, where Turkey would wield a veto in NATO's North Atlantic Council (NAC). By the end of the second round, the task force concept had been moved to the NAC and was still under discussion, although it did not appear that the initiative would be readily approved by Turkey. Turkey's team declined to contribute to the task force unless Russia was invited to participate, although it did agree to provide additional basing for antisubmarine aircraft, to invest in further Turkish naval capabilities, and to establish a NATO Center of Excellence on Black Sea Security in Istanbul. The Turkey team emphatically declined to

Figure 4.2
Russia Team Tactics by Coercion and Instrument of Power

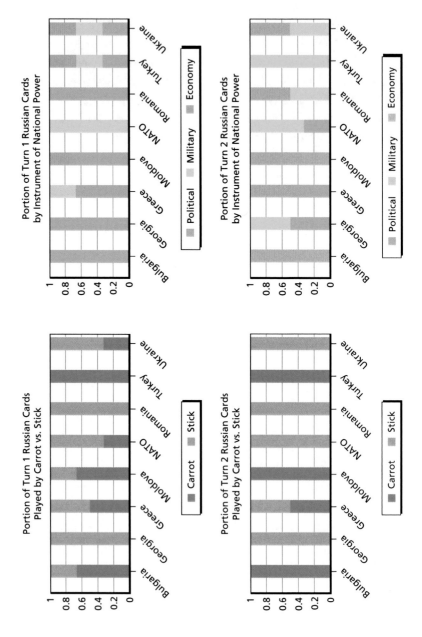

restrict Russian submarines seeking to transit back into the Black Sea from the Mediterranean.

Players representing Bulgaria presented another skeptical regional voice that sought to maintain a strong relationship with both Russia and the United States. The Bulgaria team had pledged tacit support in the NAC for the initiative but declined to publicly support it and requested additional meetings to clarify the goals of the task force and urged continued dialogue between NATO and Russia. The Bulgaria team also agreed to a summit-level meeting with Russia and proposed hosting a NATO-Russia dialogue in Sofia to address the crisis.

Moldova—which does not have veto power in the NAC or significant military capabilities to contribute to the task force—expressed its desire to expand cooperation with NATO but refused to host additional NATO special forces for training and exercises.

The remaining teams—Romania, Ukraine, Georgia, and Greece—strongly advocated an enhanced Western maritime presence in the Black Sea, consistent with Montreux provisions. These teams' starting positions were unaffected by Russian coercive actions in the military, economic, or political realm. Of these teams, Romania was the most capable of making substantial national contributions to that presence, and it pledged to contribute existing and future new vessels procured under Romania's naval modernization plan. The Romania team also issued a pledge for future national investment in additional antisubmarine warfare and air defense capabilities.[3] Teams Georgia and Ukraine both offered to host task force elements and contribute to the force as they were able but highlighted stringent limits on their capabilities and requested additional U.S. security training and assistance.

Selected moves by the three NATO allies in the Black Sea—Turkey, Bulgaria, and Romania—are displayed in Table 4.1, with a subjective assessment of the extent to which the moves supported the U.S.-led proposals within the game.

In addition to being somewhat constrained, regional team responses were directed at a variety of entities in both turns. Few

---

[3]   Jaroslaw Adamowski, "Romania to Buy 3 Sub, 4 Ships to Bolster Black Sea Ops," *Defense News*, February 9, 2018b.

Table 4.1
Moves by Regional Country Team

Country Team	Moves	Supportive?
Turkey	Support Black Sea Task Force publicly, but advocate for Russian participation and move to NATO auspices	Mixed
	Provide additional basing and port access for task force and investment in Turkish naval capabilities	Yes
	Decline to enforce Montreux Convention limiting Russian submarine return to Black Sea	No
	Pursue Black Sea Summit with Russia to resolve crisis	No
Romania	Contribute Romanian naval assets to Black Sea Task Force	Yes
	Invest in host nation infrastructure	Yes
	Provide additional naval investment	Yes
	Offer below-market reverse flows of natural gas to Bulgaria	Yes
Bulgaria	Agree not to block Black Sea Task Force in NATO, refuse public support	Mixed
	Invest in host nation infrastructure	Yes
	Agree to host additional U.S. ground forces	Yes
	Agree to bilateral meeting with Russia, offer to host NATO-Russia dialogue	No

moves were explicitly directed at the United States besides requests from Ukraine, Georgia, and Moldova for additional bilateral assistance and training. The NATO alliance received attention from teams in both turns—particularly from Romania in turn 1 and from Turkey in turn 2—but did not consistently represent a central locus of activity across the region. Instead, most moves comprised bilateral actions among partners in the region, indigenous initiatives, non-NATO multilateral contributions, and external outreach, including to the European Union and Russia. While this lack of centralized responses may have in part reflected the structure of the game, it may also accurately reflect the varied responses that Black Sea regional governments would have to an actual regional crisis, as well as the need for a flexible approach to any alliance or coalition response. Figure 4.3 illustrates the

Figure 4.3
Targets of NATO Allied and Partner Activities

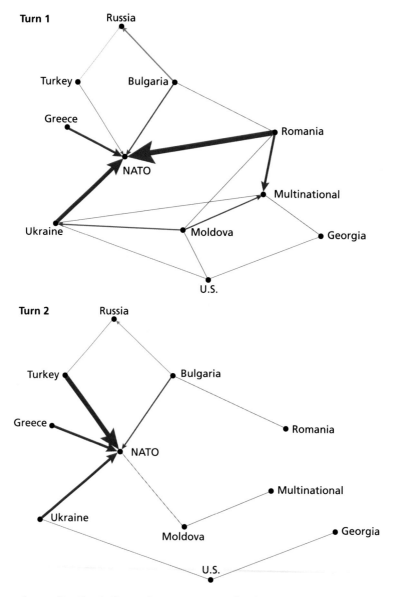

- Arrow direction indicates Source -> target of action
- Arrow thickness indicates number of interactions (min 1, max 9)
- Arrow color indicates favorability of action for NATO, with blue favoring NATO and red opposing it (subjective assessment)

dispersed nature of activities pursued by Black Sea allied and partner teams during RAND's June 2018 Black Sea game.

Ultimately, the game's outcome hinged largely on the Russian relationship with Turkey. Once a decision to develop the task force reached NATO's NAC, a decision by Turkey to block or delay the initiative would prove decisive. Russian incentives—particularly the prospect of continued enhanced cooperation in Syria and the potential costs of losing existing cooperation—appeared sufficient to give the game's Turkey pause before supporting the task force. Bilateral outreach efforts directed at Russia by the Turkey and Bulgaria teams, as well as Bulgaria's hesitation to publicly endorse the initiative, further eroded regional unity over a coherent defense and deterrence response.

CHAPTER FIVE

Conclusions

While a game—particularly a single run—may not offer decisive conclusions, RAND's Black Sea security game did highlight challenges posed by Russia's recently enhanced military position in the sea, as well as potential applications of Russian nonmilitary levers of power during a future crisis. Russia's increase in military power across the region may risk becoming a self-fulfilling prophecy. As Russia is increasingly able and willing to levy significant military costs on NATO allies and partners across the region, some governments may be deterred from responding to incremental actions that consolidate and expand the Russian position in the Black Sea. In the RAND game, even the obstruction of international freedom-of-navigation rights in Russia's expanded EEZ claims, as well as a fatal military incident stemming from Russian intimidation activities, proved largely insufficient to prompt robust regional cohesion around a military response. In light of the limitations presented by risk aversion and resource constraints, a fluid approach to coalition building—variable geometry—would likely prove necessary.

To address the intimidation of allies and partners by Russia, NATO allies and partners could take steps to negate Russia's recently gained military advantages and help reduce the military imbalance. In particular, the United States and other non–Black Sea allies should maintain—and consider expanding—the current increase in rotational naval presence in the Black Sea. While the Montreux Convention does place constraints on the timing and mass of external naval presence, allies and partners should proactively coordinate to ensure a multinational, steady state rotational presence that is consistent with the terms of Montreux.

Additional security assistance resources could also be brought to bear to bolster the capabilities of Black Sea littorals. The U.S. State Department has already sought to support Ukraine with $10 million in foreign military financing dedicated to naval resources in the wake of the November 2018 Kerch Strait incident, and it sold Ukraine two excess defense article Coast Guard vessels earlier in 2018. More recently, U.S. Congress approved a $250 million aid package for Ukraine in June 2020.[1] The United Kingdom and Lithuania have also increased contributions.[2] NATO foreign ministers pledged additional assistance to Ukraine at the December 2018 Foreign Ministerial; a consortium of the United States and other NATO allies should consider further increases in security assistance support to NATO's allies and partners in the Black Sea region, as well as the sale of excess defense articles, including destroyers, frigates, and other coastal defense assets.[3] One model for maritime assistance could be the Southeast Asia Maritime Security Initiative, for which the Department of Defense budgeted $98 million in fiscal year 2019 for equipment, supplies, and defense services, training, and small-scale construction to support the maritime security forces of five allied and partner nations in the South China Sea.[4]

The modernization of the Russian Black Sea Fleet has recently placed emphasis on new sea-based missile capabilities, increasing the risks to NATO infrastructure, equipment, and populations in the Black Sea region. Previous RAND analysis has noted that NATO

[1] Howard Altman, "$250 Million Aid Package to Ukraine Will Support U.S. Security Too," *Military Times*, June 12, 2020.

[2] "U.S. to Boost Financing for Ukraine Navy After Russian Attack," Reuters, December 21, 2018.

[3] "U.S. Eyes Giving Ukraine Oliver Hazard Perry Frigates to Boost Defenses in Black, Azov Seas," UNIAN, October 18, 2018.

[4] Office of the Secretary of Defense, *Fiscal Year 2019 President's Budget: Security Cooperation Consolidated Budget Display*, February 2018.

"missiles with a 200-kilometer range could cover the whole of the Romanian and Bulgarian coasts, as well as the Bosphorus Strait from as few as two sites," and that "deploying these missiles to bases along the length of Turkey would extend NATO anti-ship missile coverage over the whole of the Black Sea."[5] While the deployment of these missiles could prove controversial—particularly in Turkey and Bulgaria— further assessment of the political feasibility of this option should be considered.

The RAND game also highlighted the extent to which Russia's targeted application of nonmilitary sources of power could largely negate the need for it to risk explicit military conflict with NATO: the game suggested that it might well be easier for Russia to undermine regional cohesion around a unified response than for a coalition to build and maintain it. Beyond military actions, therefore, deeper understanding of the multidimensional nature of Russian instruments of power could improve efforts to preserve the independence of national decisionmaking for Black Sea allies and partners. Regular public reviews of Russian investments and other areas of financial influence in the Black Sea could offer additional transparency and provide an important starting point for political and diplomatic discussions.

In particular, the game results suggested that the United States may need to devote attention to a Black Sea security dialogue with Turkey at the senior political and military levels, despite growing political, diplomatic, and security challenges to the strategic bilateral relationship. While recognizing these areas of divergence, the United States should also acknowledge Turkey's role as a cornerstone of Black Sea security and, to the extent possible, seek to compartmentalize and depoliticize its maritime Black Sea security cooperation with Turkey. In an alliance context, one concrete mechanism through which to pursue this dialogue could be to establish a NATO Black Sea Center of Excellence in Turkey, as well as to provide the staff resources and diplomatic impetus required for it to serve as a regional intellectual hub on Black Sea security concerns. Bilaterally, the U.S.-Turkish High-Level Defense Group has previously served as a useful forum for discussion;

---

[5] Bonds et al., 2017, p. 95.

close consultations between the U.S. chairman of the Joint Chiefs of Staff and the chief of the Turkish General Staff could also be expanded to include Black Sea security if the S-400 sale is resolved in a way that permits a return to normal military relations.

More broadly, the United States should be prepared to pursue a more creative and flexible whole-of-government strategy if it seeks to foster cohesion around future regional security initiatives. To that end, several players in the RAND game emphasized the need for a robust European Union role in the Black Sea region—a point that the Romanian government has made over the past decade.[6] In the energy sphere, the United States and European Union should consider dedicated diplomatic dialogues to demonstrate support for regional initiatives to diversify supply, including regional gas interconnectors, liquefied natural gas imports, and the Trans-Anatolian Natural Gas Pipeline, in order to help ensure alternative energy options during a crisis.

Proactive efforts to address creeping Russian monopolization of regional media outlets would help to undercut Russian disinformation platforms. Previous studies have recommended that the U.S. government prioritize support for investigative journalism and media independence in Eastern Europe: such action would be of particular strategic significance in the Black Sea region and should also be prioritized by the European Union.[7] The U.S. State Department's Global Engagement Center could play a constructive role in tracking and exposing sources of Russian media influence in the Black Sea region, as could NATO's Strategic Communications Centre of Excellence.[8]

Finally, but importantly, continued U.S. and European engagement with Georgia and Ukraine will be critical to demonstrate to these partner governments and populations—as well as to Russia—that their independence and security remain a priority. In particular, the United States should consider revisiting existing bilateral trade agreements to more closely reflect the trade relationships offered by the European Union's Deep and Comprehensive Free Trade Area agreement with

---

[6] Joja, 2018.

[7] Conley and Ruy, 2018.

[8] Costello, 2018.

both countries.[9] In the security sphere, while NATO membership may not be a viable near-term prospect for Georgia and Ukraine, it should remain an option for the medium and long term, in the words of former NATO secretary general Alexander Vershbow, "both as a matter of principle and because the freedom to choose one's security arrangements is enshrined in the Helsinki Final Act, a document that Russia helped write."[10]

Ultimately the RAND game underscored the need for robust analysis surrounding further efforts toward enhanced defense and deterrence options in the Black Sea. A shifting regional military balance has altered the security landscape; the presence of three allies and two partners in the region makes that security landscape of clear interest to the United States. Given the extensive Russian military activities, investment, and political priorities in the Black Sea, Russia's 2018 actions in the Kerch Strait were unsurprising, if unequivocally illegal. As Western allies and partners continue longer-term responses to the event, it would be wise to lay the groundwork early to prepare for future Black Sea military crises that could well arise.

---

[9] Tony Barber, "Ukraine Reaps Benefits of Trade Deal with EU," *Financial Times*, September 11, 2018.

[10] Alexander Vershbow, "Black Sea Is Where Russia's Aggression Against Ukraine Began," remarks to the NATO Parliamentary Assembly, July 4, 2017.

References

Adamowski, Jaroslaw, "Romania Inks $1B Deal for Hundreds of Infantry Fighting Vehicles," *Defense News*, January 12, 2018a.

———, "Romania to Buy 3 Sub, 4 Ships to Bolster Black Sea Ops," *Defense News*, February 9, 2018b.

———, "Saab, Diehl Defence Team Up to Offer Missile to Romanian, Bulgarian Navies," *Defense News*, September 4, 2019a.

———, "Romania, Bulgaria Boost Defense Buys Amid Fear of Russia," *Defense News*, September 8, 2019b.

"Admiral Bülent Bostanoglu, Commander, Turkish Navy," *Jane's Defence Weekly*, May 27, 2015.

"After Calls for Black Sea FONOPS, US to Support Ukraine Navy with $10m Investment," *Naval Today*, December 24, 2018.

Altman, Howard, "$250 Million Aid Package to Ukraine Will Support US Security Too, Defense Experts Say," *Military Times*, June 12, 2020.

Antonenko, Anton, Roman Nitsovych, Olena Pavlenko, and Krisitan Takac, "Reforming Ukraine's Energy Sector: Critical Unfinished Business," *Carnegie Europe, Reforming Ukraine Project*, February 6, 2018. As of July 17, 2019: https://carnegieeurope.eu/2018/02/06/reforming-ukraine-s-energy-sector-critical -unfinished-business-pub-75449

Associated Press, "Russia Places Sanctions on Turkey," *New York Times*, November 28, 2015.

———, "Romania Minister Says Country Facing Cyber-Attacks, Russian," *Voice of America*, June 25, 2018. As of July 17, 2019: https://www.voanews.com/a/romania-minister-says-country-facing-cyber-attacks -russians/4453420.html

———, "Russia, Turkey Mull Next Steps in War-Torn Syria," *Voice of America*, January 23, 2019. As of July 17, 2019: https://www.voanews.com/europe/russia-turkey-mull-next-steps-war-torn-syria

Barber, Tony, "Ukraine Reaps Benefits of Trade Deal with EU," *Financial Times*, September 11, 2018.

Barnes, Julian, "A Russian Ghost Submarine, Its U.S. Pursuers and a Deadly New Cold War," *Wall Street Journal*, October 20, 2017.

Batashvili, David, "Russia Troop Deployments Menace Georgia," *Civil.ge*, April 4, 2017. As of July 15, 2019:
https://old.civil.ge/eng/article.php?id=29994

Bechev, Dimitar, *Russia's Influence in Bulgaria*, Brussels: New Direction, May 12, 2015. As of July 17, 2019:
https://europeanreform.org/files/ND-report-RussiasInfluenceInBulgaria-preview-lo-res_FV.pdf

———, *Rival Power: Russia in Southeast Europe*, New Haven, Conn.: Yale University Press, 2017.

———, "Bulgaria," in Oana Popescu and Rufin Zamfir, eds., *Propaganda Made-to-Measure: How Our Vulnerabilities Facilitate Russian Influence*, Bucharest: Global Focus, 2018, pp. 132–161.

———, "Turkey and Black Sea Security: Ten Years After the War in Georgia," *New Atlanticist* (Atlantic Council blog), August 8, 2018. As of July 15, 2019:
https://www.atlanticcouncil.org/blogs/new-atlanticist/turkey-and-black-sea-security-ten-years-after-the-war-in-georgia

———, "Russia's Pipe Dreams Are Europe's Nightmare," *Foreign Policy*, March 12, 2019.

Bekdil, Burak Ege, "Turkish Shipyards Join Forces to Develop First Locally Made Ship Engine," *Defense News*, April 16, 2018. As of July 17, 2019:
https://www.defensenews.com/naval/2018/04/16/turkish-shipyards-join-forces-to-develop-engine/

Bender, Georgiana, "Cyber Attack on Romanian Institution Foiled by Intelligence Services," *Business Review*, May 12, 2017. As of July 15, 2019:
http://business-review.eu/news/cyber-attack-on-romanian-institution-foiled-by-intelligence-services-137657

Bhalla, Reva, "Turkey's Time Has Come," *Real Clear World*, December 10, 2015.

"Black Sea Oil & Gas to Go Ahead with $400 Million Romanian Offshore Project," Reuters, February 6, 2019. As of July 17, 2019:
https://www.reuters.com/article/us-romania-energy-gas/black-sea-oil-gas-to-go-ahead-with-400-million-romanian-offshore-project-idUSKCN1PW0M1

"The Black Sea Region: A Critical Intersection," *NATO Review*, May 25, 2018.

Blank, Stephen, "How the US Can Shore Up Ukraine's Vulnerabilities in the Black Sea," *UkraineAlert* (Atlantic Council blog), March 21, 2018. As of July 15, 2019:
https://www.atlanticcouncil.org/blogs/ukrainealert/how-the-us-can-shore-up-ukraine-s-vulnerabilities-in-the-black-sea

Boltenkov, Dmitry, "Reform of the Russian Navy," in Mikhail Barabanov, ed., *Russia's New Army*, Moscow: Center for Analysis of Strategies and Technologies, 2011, pp. 81–101.

Bonds, Timothy M., Joel B. Predd, Timothy R. Heath, Michael S. Chase, Michael Johnson, Michael J. Lostumbo, James Bonomo, Muharrem Mane, and Paul S. Steinberg, *What Role Can Land-Based, Multi-Domain Anti-Access/Area Denial Forces Play in Deterring or Defeating Aggression?* Santa Monica, Calif.: RAND Corporation, RR-1820-A, 2017. As of July 8, 2019:
https://www.rand.org/pubs/research_reports/RR1820.html

"British Jets Scramble from Romania to Investigate Russian Fighter Jets," *Radio Free Europe/Radio Liberty*, August 22, 2018. As of July 17, 2019:
https://www.rferl.org/a/british-jets-scramble-from-romania-to-investigate-russian
-fighter-jets/29447745.html

Broad, William J., "In Taking Crimea, Putin Gains a Sea of Fuel Reserves," *New York Times*, May 17, 2014.

Browne, Ryan, "US Show of Force Sends Russia a Message in Black Sea," *CNN*, February 20, 2018.

"Bulgarian-Hosted Exercise Breeze 2018 Concludes," *Naval Today*, July 24, 2018. As of July 17, 2019:
https://navaltoday.com/2018/07/24/bulgarian-hosted-exercise-breeze-2018-concludes/

"Bulgarian President Radev Blames Ukraine for Kerch Straits Crisis," *Sofia Globe*, November 30, 2018. As of July 17, 2019:
https://sofiaglobe.com/2018/11/30/bulgarian-president-radev-blames-ukraine-for
-kerch-straits-crisis/

"Bulgaria Says Will Not Expel Russian Diplomats over Spy Poisoning," Reuters, March 30, 2018.

"Bulgaria Says Will Not Join Any NATO Black Sea Fleet After Russian Warning," Reuters, June 16, 2016. As of July 17, 2019:
https://www.reuters.com/article/nato-bulgaria-blacksea-idUSL8N19835X

"Bulgaria Seeks Funding for Second Nuclear Power Plant," *Radio Free Europe/Radio Liberty*, March 11, 2019.

"Bulgaria to Build New Link to Turkey in Hope of Russian Gas," Reuters, June 26, 2018.

"Bulgaria to Buy Eight New F-16s from US," *Emerging Europe*, January 10, 2019.

Cagaptay, Soner, and James F. Jeffrey, "Turkey's Muted Reaction to the Crimean Crisis," *Washington Institute*, March 4, 2014. As of July 17, 2019:
https://www.washingtoninstitute.org/policy-analysis/view/turkeys-muted-reaction
-to-the-crimean-crisis

Chiriac, Marian, "Romania Defiant over Russian Gas Squeeze," *Balkan Insight*, September 16, 2014. As of July 17, 2019:
https://balkaninsight.com/2014/09/16/russian-gas-cut-off-not-to-affect-romania/

Cholakov, Peter, "Russia's Proposed TurkStream 2 Pipeline Sparks Bulgaria, EU Energy Worries," *Die Welt*, February 28, 2019.

Clark, David, "Ukraine's Economy Has Turned a Corner," *Financial Times*, July 4, 2017.

Cohen, Raphael S., and Andrew Radin, *Russia's Hostile Measures in Europe: Understanding the Threat*, Santa Monica, Calif.: RAND Corporation, RR-1793-A, 2019. As of September 17, 2019:
https://www.rand.org/pubs/research_reports/RR1793.html

Cohen, Zachary, and Ryan Browne, "US Military Flexes Muscles in Message to Russia," *CNN*, December 6, 2018.

Conley, Heather A., and Donatienne Ruy, "Kremlin Playbook: Spotlight Moldova," *Center for Strategic and International Studies*, July 19, 2018. As of July 16, 2019:
https://www.csis.org/blogs/kremlin-playbook-spotlight/kremlin-playbook-spotlight-moldova

Conley, Heather A., James Mina, Ruslan Stefanov, and Martin Vladimirov, *The Kremlin Playbook: Understanding Russian Influence in Central and Eastern Europe*, report of the Center for Strategic and International Studies Europe Program and the Center for the Study of Democracy Economics Program, Lanham, Md.: Rowman and Littlefield, October 2016.

Convention Regarding the Regime of the Straits, signed in Montreux, Switzerland, July 20, 1936.

"Convention Regarding the Regime of the Straits," *American Journal of International Law*, Vol. 31, No. 1, 1937, pp. 1–18.

Costello, Katherine, *Russia's Use of Media and Information Operations in Turkey: Implications for the United States*, Santa Monica, Calif.: RAND Corporation, PE-278-A, 2018. As of July 15, 2019:
https://www.rand.org/pubs/perspectives/PE278.html

Cranny-Evans, Samuel, "Russia's Southern Military District Receives Mechanized, Airmobile Reinforcements," *Jane's Defence Weekly*, December 5, 2018.

Daiss, Tim, "Ukraine Celebration: One Year Without Russian Gas," *Forbes*, November 27, 2016. As of July 15, 2019:
https://www.forbes.com/sites/timdaiss/2016/11/27/ukraine-celebration-one-year-without-russian-gas/#5a4a31ed62f4

Dalsjo, Robert, Christofer Berglund, and Michael Jonsson, *Bursting the Bubble: Russian A2/AD in the Baltic Sea Region: Capabilities, Countermeasures, and Implications*, Stockholm: Swedish Defence Research Agency, March 2019.

De Carbonnel, Alissa, and Tsvetelia Tsolov, "Old Ties with Russia Weigh on Bulgarian Decision in Spy Poisoning Case," Reuters, March 29, 2018.

Delanoe, Igor, "After the Crimean Crisis: Towards a Greater Russian Maritime Power in the Black Sea," *Southeast European and Black Sea Studies*, Vol. 14, No. 3, 2014, pp. 367–382.

Dettmer, Jamie, "NATO Commander Warns of Crimea 'Militarization,'" *Voice of America*, November 26, 2014.

Dickstein, Corey, "Pentagon: Russian Aircraft Flew Too Close to US Destroyer in Black Sea," *Stars and Stripes*, February 14, 2017. As of July 17, 2019: https://www.stripes.com/news/pentagon-russian-aircraft-flew-too-close-to-us -destroyer-in-black-sea-1.454009

Dyomkin, Denis, "Russia Says Georgia War Stopped NATO Expansion," Reuters, November 21, 2011.

———, "Putin Says Romania, Poland, May Now Be in Russia's Cross-Hairs," Reuters, May 27, 2016.

Dyson, Tauren, "Raytheon to Supply Romania with Missile Defense Systems," *UPI*, November 4, 2018.

Eckstein, Megan, "U.S. Navy Command Ship, Destroyer in Black Sea for Annual Sea Breeze Exercise," *USNI News*, July 10, 2018.

"Erdogan May Have Politicized Issue of Russian Gas Prices to Send a Signal to US—Expert," TASS, April 10, 2019. As of July 17, 2019: http://tass.com/world/1052963

"Erdogan Warns NATO Black Sea Has Become 'Russian Lake,'" *B92*, May 12, 2016.

Esipova, Neli, and Julie Ray, "Eastern Europeans, CIS Residents See Russia, U.S. as Threats," *Gallup*, April 4, 2016.

European Commission, "State Aid: Commission Approves Public Support for Natural Gas Interconnector Between Greece and Bulgaria," press release, European Union, Brussels, November 8, 2018. As of July 15, 2019: http://europa.eu/rapid/press-release_IP-18-6342_en.htm

Fiorentino, Michael-Ross, "PM Borissov Assures NATO Bulgaria Is Not Russia's 'Trojan Horse,'" *Euronews*, February 3, 2019. As of July 15, 2019: https://www.euronews.com/2019/03/02/pm-borissov-assures-nato-bulgaria-is-not -russia-s-trojan-horse

Galeotti, Mark, *Russian Political War: Moving Beyond the Hybrid*, London: Routledge, 2019.

Gall, Carlotta, "President Recep Tayyip Erdogan of Turkey Replaces Top Military Chiefs," *New York Times*, August 2, 2017.

"General Staff: Russia-Turkey Balance of Force in Black Sea Has Changed over Years," TASS, September 14, 2016.

Georgian Ministry of Foreign Affairs, *Quarterly Report on Human Rights Abuses in the Occupied Territories*, January 2016.

Gerit, Selin, "Turkey Faces Big Losses as Russia Sanctions Bite," *BBC*, January 6, 2016. As of July 17, 2019:
https://www.bbc.com/news/world-europe-35209987

Gherasim, Cristian, "After 22 Years, Romania's Navy Is Aiming Beneath the Waves Again," *Euronews*, January 20, 2018. As of July 15, 2019:
https://www.euronews.com/2018/01/30/after-22-years-romania-s-navy-is-aiming -beneath-the-waves-again

Gibbons-Neff, Thomas, "Top NATO General: Russians Starting to Build Air Defense Bubble over Syria," *Washington Post*, September 29, 2015.

Gorenburg, Dmitry, "Black Sea Fleet Projects Power Westwards," *Oxford Analytica*, April 2016a.

———, "Black Sea Fleet Projects Power Westwards," *Russian Military Reform* blog, July 20, 2016b. As of July 15, 2019:
https://russiamil.wordpress.com/2016/07/20/black-sea-fleet-projects-power-westwards/

———, "Is a New Russian Black Sea Fleet Coming? Or Is It Here?" *War on the Rocks*, July 31, 2018.

Gotev, Georgi, "Bulgaria Refuses to Join NATO Black Sea Fleet Against Russia," *Euractiv*, June 16, 2016. As of July 15, 2019:
https://www.euractiv.com/section/global-europe/news/bulgaria-refuses-to-join -nato-black-sea-fleet-against-russia/

———, "At EU Summit, Borissov Deplores 'Terrible' Russian Cyberattacks on Bulgaria," *Euractiv*, October 18, 2018. As of July 17, 2019:
https://www.euractiv.com/section/defence-and-security/news/at-eu-summit -borissov-deplores-terrible-russian-cyberattacks-on-bulgaria/

Grant, Glen, "Real Action Is Now Needed in the Azov Sea," *Kyiv Post*, August 20, 2018.

Grigas, Agnia, *Beyond Crimea: The New Russian Empire*, New Haven, Conn.: Yale University Press, 2016.

Gurzu, Anca, "Romania's Black Sea Gas Sparks Political Crisis," *Politico*, August 23, 2018. As of July 17, 2019:
https://www.politico.eu/article/romania-black-sea-gas-political-crisis-liviu-dragnea/

Hanlon, Bradley, and Alexander Roberds, "Securing Bulgaria's Future: Combating Russian Energy Influence in the Balkans," *Alliance for Securing Democracy*, June 21, 2018. As of July 17, 2019:
https://securingdemocracy.gmfus.org/securing-bulgarias-future-combating-russian -energy-influence-in-the-balkans/

Hedenskog, Jakob, Erika Holmquist, and Johan Norberg, *Security in the Caucasus: Russian Policy and Military Posture*, Stockholm: Swedish Defence Research Agency, 2018.

Higgens, Andrew, "Russia Slowly Throttles a Ukrainian Port," *New York Times*, December 14, 2018. As of July 17, 2019:
https://www.nytimes.com/2018/12/14/world/europe/moscow-ukraine-azov
-mariupol.html

Hill, Fiona, "Beyond Co-Dependency: European Reliance on Russian Energy," *Brookings Institution*, July 1, 2005. As of July 17, 2019:
https://www.brookings.edu/research/beyond-co-dependency-european-reliance
-on-russian-energy/

Hill, Fiona, and Omer Taspinar, "Turkey and Russia: The Axis of the Excluded?" *Survival*, Vol. 48, No. 1, 2006, pp. 81–92.

"Implementation of the Montreux Convention," *Turkish Ministry of Foreign Affairs*, undated. As of April 24, 2019:
http://www.mfa.gov.tr/implementation-of-the-montreux-convention.en.mfa

"In Crimea, Russia Signals Military Resolve with New and Revamped Bases," Reuters, November 1, 2016.

International Institute for Strategic Studies, *The Military Balance 2010*, London: Routledge for the International Institute for Strategic Studies, 2010.

———, *The Military Balance 2018*, London: Routledge for the International Institute for Strategic Studies, 2018.

———, *The Military Balance 2019*, London: Routledge for the International Institute for Strategic Studies, 2019.

Johnston, Robert, "Russia Ramps Up Cyber Warfare as It Loses Economic Footing in Ukraine," *The Hill*, December 13, 2018.

Joja, Iulia-Sabina, "Dealing with the Russian Lake Next Door: Romania and Black Sea Security," *War on the Rocks*, August 15, 2018.

Jones, Bruce, "Ukraine Reinforces Its Presence in Azov Sea," *Jane's Navy International*, September 13, 2018.

Judson, Jen, "Romania Signs Off on US Deal to Become First European HIMARS Customer," *Defense News*, February 28, 2018.

Kapanadze, Sergi, *Georgia's Vulnerability to Russian Pressure Points*, London: European Council on Foreign Relations, June 2014. As of July 17, 2019:
https://www.ecfr.eu/page/-/ECFR106_GEORGIA_MEMO_AW.pdf

Karamanau, Yuras, and Vladimir Isachenkov, "Ukraine Urges NATO to Deploy Ships in Dispute with Russia," Associated Press, November 29, 2018. As of July 17, 2019:
https://www.apnews.com/ec0dfbf8d8b94eb6983e9054e2a808c7

Kremlin Watch Team, *Kremlin Influence in the Visegrad Countries and Romania*, Kremlin Watch memo, European Values Think-Tank and Wilfried Martens Centre for European Studies, October 23, 2017. As of July 17, 2019: https://www.europeanvalues.net/wp-content/uploads/2017/12/Kremlin-Influence-in-Visegrad-Countries-and-Romania.pdf

Kucera, Joshua, "Romania Pushing for Permanent NATO Presence in Black Sea," *Eurasianet*, January 18, 2016a. As of July 15, 2019: https://eurasianet.org/romania-pushing-for-permanent-nato-presence-in-black-sea

———, "Russia Claims 'Mastery' over Turkey in Black Sea," *Eurasianet*, September 25, 2016b. As of July 15, 2019: https://eurasianet.org/russia-claims-mastery-over-turkey-black-sea

Kuimova, Alexandra, and Seimon T. Wezeman, *Georgia and Black Sea Security*, SIPRI Background Paper, Solna, Sweden: Stockholm International Peace Research Institute, December 2018a. As of July 17, 2019: https://www.sipri.org/sites/default/files/2018-12/bp_1812_black_sea_georgia_0.pdf

———, *Russia and Black Sea Security*, SIPRI Background Paper, Solna, Sweden: Stockholm International Peace Research Institute, December 2018b. As of July 16, 2019: https://www.sipri.org/sites/default/files/2018-12/bp_1812_black_sea_russia_0.pdf

Kurtdarcan, Bleda, and Barın Kayaoğlu, "Russia, Turkey and the Black Sea A2/AD Arms Race," *National Interest*, March 5, 2017. As of July 15, 2019: https://nationalinterest.org/feature/russia-turkey-the-black-sea-a2-ad-arms-race-19673

LaGrone, Sam, "USS *Porter* Buzzed by Russian Planes in Black Sea," *USNI News*, February 14, 2017.

———, "Russians Use U.S. Navy's Aegis Ashore as Excuse to Deploy Strategic Bombers to Crimea," *USNI News*, March 18, 2019.

Larrabee, F. Stephen, and Stephen J. Flanagan, "The Growing Importance of Black Sea Security," *U.S. News and World Report*, July 11, 2016.

Larrabee, F. Stephen, Stephanie Pezard, Andrew Radin, Nathan Chandler, Keith Crane, and Thomas S. Szayna, *Russia and the West After the Ukrainian Crisis: European Vulnerabilities to Russian Pressures*, Santa Monica, Calif.: RAND Corporation, RR-1305-A, 2017. As of July 15, 2019: https://www.rand.org/pubs/research_reports/RR1305.html

Larter, David B., and Matthew Bodner, "The Sea of Azov Won't Become the New South China Sea (and Russia Knows It)," *Defense News*, November 28, 2018.

Litovkin, Nikolai, "'Black Hole': What Makes Russia's Newest Submarine Unique?" *Russia Beyond the Headlines*, November 29, 2016.

Lomidze, Irakli, "Cyber Attacks Against Georgia," briefing slides, Tbilisi, Georgia: Ministry of Justice of Georgia, Data Exchange Agency, 2011.

Luca, Ana Maria, "US Plans to Upgrade Military Bases in Romania, Bulgaria," *Balkan Insight*, August 15, 2018.

Majumdar, Dave, "Why Are Russia and Turkey Holding Joint Naval Exercises in the Black Sea?" *National Interest*, April 5, 2017.

———, "All Is Not Well with Russia's Black Sea Fleet," *National Interest*, June 20, 2018.

Mammadova, Leman, "Bulgaria Eyes to Receive Additional Gas from Azerbaijan," *Azernews*, March 15, 2019. As of July 17, 2019:
https://www.azernews.az/oil_and_gas/147356.html

Mankoff, Jeffrey, "A Friend in Need? Russia and Turkey After the Coup," *Center for Strategic and International Studies*, July 29, 2016. As of July 17, 2019:
https://www.csis.org/analysis/friend-need-russia-and-turkey-after-coup

Martin, Nik, "TurkStream: Who Profits, Who Loses Out?" *Die Welt*, November 19, 2018.

McLeary, Paul, "With Demands for More NATO Spending, Romania Steps Up," *The Cable, Foreign Policy*, May 3, 2017.

"Meet Russia's Tu-22M3 Backfire, the Bomber That Could Sink a Navy Aircraft Carrier," *National Interest*, June 5, 2018.

Melenciuc, Sorin, "Romania's Military Spending Rose 50 pct to USD 4 bln in 2017, the Biggest Increase in the World," *Business Review*, March 5, 2018. As of July 15, 2019:
http://business-review.eu/news/romanias-military-spending-rose-50-pct-to-usd-4-bln-in-2017-the-biggest-increase-in-the-world-167662

Melvin, Neil, *Rebuilding Collective Security in the Black Sea*, Solna, Sweden: Stockholm International Peace Research Institute, SIPRI Policy Paper 50, December 2018.

Menabde, Giorgi, "Russian Military Absorbs 'Army of South Ossetia,'" *Eurasia Daily Monitor*, March 21, 2017. As of July 16, 2019:
https://jamestown.org/program/russian-military-absorbs-army-south-ossetia/

Mikhelidze, Nona, and Nathalie Tocci, "Europe's Russia Sanctions Are Not Working," *Politico*, November 28, 2018.

Minich, Ruslan, "Russia Shows Its Military Might in the Black Sea and Beyond," *UkraineAlert* (Atlantic Council blog), November 6, 2018. As of July 15, 2019:
https://www.atlanticcouncil.org/blogs/ukrainealert/russia-shows-its-military-might-in-the-black-sea-and-beyond

Morrison, Thea, "Georgia Not to Purchase Gas from Russia in 2018," *Georgia Today*, January 9, 2018.

Munoz, Carlo, "Bulgaria Approves $1.4 Billion for New Warships, Fighters" *UPI*, April 5, 2016.

"NATO Groups in Black Sea Make Port Calls in Bulgaria," *Naval Today*, February 12, 2018.

Necsutu, Madalin, "Moldova, Romania Boost Military Cooperation with Joint Battalion," *Balkan Insight*, February 6, 2018. As of July 17, 2019: https://balkaninsight.com/2018/02/06/romania-russia-strengthen-defence -influence-in-divided-moldova-02-06-2018/

"The New Kids on the Block," *The Economist*, January 4, 2007. As of July 17, 2019: https://www.economist.com/europe/2007/01/04/the-new-kids-on-the-block

Newnham, Randall, "Oil, Carrots, and Sticks: Russia's Energy Resources as a Foreign Policy Tool," *Journal of Eurasian Studies*, Vol. 2, No. 2, 2011, pp. 134–143.

Nichol, Jim, *Russia-Georgia Conflict in August 2008: Context and Implications for U.S. Interests*, Washington, D.C.: Congressional Research Service, CRS Report RL34618, March 3, 2009. As of July 17, 2019: https://fas.org/sgp/crs/row/RL34618.pdf

Nieczypor, Krzysztof, "A Closely Watched Basin: The Russian–Ukrainian Tensions in the Sea of Azov," *Centre for Eastern Studies*, August 8, 2018. As of July 15, 2019: https://www.osw.waw.pl/en/publikacje/osw-commentary/2018-08-08/a-closely -watched-basin-russian-ukrainian-tensions-sea-azov-0

Office of the Secretary of Defense, *Fiscal Year 2019 President's Budget: Security Cooperation Consolidated Budget Display*, February 2018. As of July 15, 2019: https://comptroller.defense.gov/Portals/45/Documents/defbudget/fy2019/ Security_Cooperation_Budget_Display_OUSDC.pdf

Panda, Ankit, "US Navy Conducts First Post–Cold War FONOP in Peter the Great Bay, Off Russian Coast," *The Diplomat*, December 6, 2018.

Parkinson, Joe, and Georgi Kantchev, "Document: Russia Uses Rigged Polls, Fake News to Sway Foreign Elections," *Wall Street Journal*, March 23, 2017.

"Personal Remittances Received—Georgia," *World Bank Group*, 2019. As of July 15, 2019: https://data.worldbank.org/indicator/BX.TRF.PWKR.DT.GD.ZS?locations=GE

Peterson, Michael, "The Naval Power Shift in the Black Sea," *War on the Rocks*, January 9, 2019.

Pew Research Center, "Views on Role of Russia in the Region, and the Soviet Union," chapter 7 in *Religious Belief and National Belonging in Central and Eastern Europe*, Washington, D.C., May 10, 2017.

Polityuk, Pavel, and Natalia Zinets, "Pledging Reforms by 2020, Ukraine Seeks Route into NATO," Reuters, July 10, 2017.

Ponomarenko, Illia, "Ukraine Accepts Two US Patrol Boats After 4 Years of Bureaucratic Blockades," *Kyiv Post*, September 27, 2018.

Popescu, Oana, and Rufin Zamfir, eds., *Propaganda Made-to-Measure: How Our Vulnerabilities Facilitate Russian Influence*, Bucharest: Global Focus Asymmetric Threats Programme, February 2018.

"Public Opinion of the Population of Ukraine on NATO," *Ilko Kucheriv Democratic Initiatives Foundation*, July 5, 2017. As of July 15, 2019: https://dif.org.ua/en/article/public-opinion-of-the-population-of-ukraine-on-nato

Rebegea, Corina, "Living the Russian Dream," brief, *Center for European Policy Analysis*, July 19, 2017. As of July 15, 2019: http://infowar.cepa.org/Briefs/Ro/Living-the-Russian-dream

Rempfer, Kyle, "Here's the US Military Footprint in the Black Sea Region," *Military Times*, November 27, 2018a.

———, "Why Russia Is Swallowing the Black Sea and Won't Stop Until It Has 'Choked Out Ukraine,'" *Military Times*, December 31, 2018b.

Republic of Turkey Ministry of Energy and Natural Resources, "Natural Gas Pipelines and Projects," 2019. As of June 17, 2019: https://www.enerji.gov.tr/en-us/pages/natural-gas-pipelines-and-projects

Roblin, Sebastien, "Introducing Russia's 5 Deadliest Warships in the Black Sea," *National Interest*, December 1, 2018.

"Romanian Parliament Says Would Back Reunification with Moldova," Reuters, March 27, 2018.

"Romania Says Its Natural Gas Output Set to Double by 2025," Reuters, February 20, 2018. As of July 17, 2019: https://www.reuters.com/article/romania-energy-gas/corrected-update-1-romania -says-its-natural-gas-output-set-to-double-by-2025-idUSL8N1QA3ZH

"Romania Suspends EUR 1.6b Corvette Tender," *Naval Today*, January 14, 2019.

"Romania Wants Russia to Explain Official's Threatening Remarks," *Radio Free Europe/Radio Liberty*, May 11, 2014.

"Russia and Turkey Will Both Lose from Moscow's Sanctions," *CNN*, November 30, 2015.

"Russia Expands Military Exercises to 80,000 Troops," Agence France-Presse, March 19, 2015.

"Russia: Georgia's Largest Source of Remittances," *Georgia Today*, January 20, 2018. As of July 17, 2019: http://georgiatoday.ge/news/8817/Russia%3A-Georgia's-largest-source-of-remittances

"Russia May Give Turkey 10 Percent Gas Price Reduction—Report," *Ahval*, April 10, 2019. As of July 17, 2019: https://ahvalnews.com/turkey-russia/russia-may-give-turkey-10-percent-gas-price -reduction-report

"Russian General Says Kremlin Deploys Air-Defense Missiles in Abkhazia," *Radio Free Europe/Radio Liberty*, August 11, 2010.

"Russia to Reinforce Black Sea Fleet with Bastion Missile Systems," *UAWire*, March 4, 2019.

"Russia Warns NATO Not to Build Up Naval Forces in Black Sea," Reuters, June 15, 2016. As of July 17, 2019:
https://uk.reuters.com/article/uk-nato-russia-blacksea/russia-warns-nato-not-to-build-up-naval-forces-in-black-sea-idUKKCN0Z11SF

Rzayeva, Gulmira, *Gas Supply Changes in Turkey*, Oxford: Oxford Institute for Energy Studies, January 2018. As of July 17, 2019:
https://www.oxfordenergy.org/wpcms/wp-content/uploads/2018/01/Gas-Supply-Changes-in-Turkey-Insight-24.pdf

Sanders, Deborah, "The Crimean Crisis and Russia's Maritime Power in the Black Sea," *Defence-in-Depth* blog, October 27, 2014. As of July 15, 2019:
https://defenceindepth.co/2014/10/27/the-crimean-crisis-and-russias-maritime-power-in-the-black-sea/

———, *Maritime Power in the Black Sea*, London: Routledge, 2016.

———, "Rebuilding the Ukrainian Navy," *Naval War College Review*, Vol. 70, No. 4, 2017, pp. 61–77. As of July 16, 2019:
https://digital-commons.usnwc.edu/nwc-review/vol70/iss4/5/

Scott, Richard, and Luca Peruzzi, "Romania Set to Choose Four New Corvettes, Frigate Upgrade," *Jane's 360*, October 22, 2018.

Schneider, Alex, "Russia's Black Sea Fleet Buildup," *The Maritime Executive,* March 29 2017.

Simmons, Jo, "The Curious Tale of Bulgaria's Extremist Flip-Flopping Party," *Huffington Post*, June 3, 2014. As of July 17, 2019:
https://www.huffingtonpost.co.uk/jo-simmons/volen-siderov-ataka_b_5432359.html

Smith, Julianne, and Jerry Hendrix, *Forgotten Waters: Minding the GIUK Gap*, tabletop exercise report, Washington, D.C.: Center for New American Security, May 2, 2017. As of July 16, 2019:
https://www.cnas.org/publications/reports/forgotten-waters

Sloat, Amanda, "Turkey Wants to Crush U.S. Allies in Syria. That Shouldn't Surprise Anybody," *Order from Chaos* (Brookings Institution blog), January 24, 2018. As of July 15, 2019:
https://www.brookings.edu/blog/order-from-chaos/2018/01/24/turkey-wants-to-crush-us-allies-in-syria-that-shouldnt-surprise-anybody/

"Shrinking the Black Sea," *The Economist*, February 16, 2019.

Snow, Shawn, "No More Marine Rotations to the Black Sea. The Corps Is Focusing Here Instead," *Marine Corps Times*, November 29, 2018.

Stronski, Paul, and Annie Himes, *Russia's Game in the Balkans*, working paper, Washington, D.C.: Carnegie Endowment for International Peace, January 2019.

Sutton, H. I., "Turkey's New Assault Carrier Will Transform Navy," *Forbes*, May 13, 2020.

Thatcher, Chris, "RCAF Hornets Intercept Russian Su-27 Flanker," October 26, 2018. As of July 22, 2019:
https://www.skiesmag.com/news/rcaf-hornets-intercept-russian-su-27-flanker/

Tian, Nan, Aude Fleurant, Alexandra Kuimova, Pieter D. Wezeman, and Siemon T. Wezeman, *Trends in World Military Expenditure, 2017*, fact sheet, Solna, Sweden: Stockholm International Peace Research Institute, May 2018. As of July 15, 2019:
https://www.sipri.org/publications/2018/sipri-fact-sheets/trends-world-military
-expenditure-2017

Toucas, Boris, "NATO and Russia in the Black Sea: A New Confrontation?" *Center for Strategic and International Studies*, March 6, 2017. As of July 16, 2019:
https://www.csis.org/analysis/nato-and-russia-black-sea-new-confrontation

Tsiboukis, George, "Bulgarian Navy Corvette Procurement Is Back On," *Defense IQ*, October 2, 2017. As of July 17, 2019:
https://www.defenceiq.com/naval-maritime-defence/news/bulgarian-navy-corvette
-procurement-is-back-on

"Turkey and Azerbaijan Mark Completion of TANAP Pipeline to Take Gas to Europe," *Reuters*, November 30, 2019.

"Turkey Hits Historic LNG Import Record in Jan," *Hurriyet Daily News*, March 30, 2019.

"Turkey Opens TANAP Pipeline That Will Bring Azeri Gas to Europe," *Die Welt*, June 12, 2018.

"Ukraine President Signs Constitutional Amendment on NATO, EU Membership," *Radio Free Europe/Radio Liberty*, February 19, 2019.

U.S. Defense Intelligence Agency, *Russia Military Power: Building a Military to Support Great Power Aspirations*, Washington, D.C., 2017.

U.S. Energy Information Administration, *Country Analysis Brief: Turkey*, Washington, D.C., February 2, 2017.

"U.S. Eyes Giving Ukraine Oliver Hazard Perry Frigates to Boost Defenses in Black, Azov Seas," UNIAN, October 18, 2018.

"U.S. to Boost Financing for Ukraine Navy After Russian Attack," Reuters, December 21, 2018.

"U.S. Warship Arrives at Romanian Port amid Black Sea Tensions," *Radio Free Europe/Radio Liberty*, January 8, 2019.

Uver, Akin, "Ankara to Black Sea: Turkey and Russia's Age-Old Struggle for Regional Supremacy," *Foreign Affairs*, May 12, 2014.

Vandiver, John, "Air Force Wants to Turn Soviet-Era Base in Romania into NATO Black Sea Hub," *Stars and Stripes*, July 9, 2020.

Vergun, David, "U.S. Soldiers in Bulgaria, Romania Deter Aggression, Assure Allies," *Army News Service*, September 26, 2017.

Vershbow, Alexander, "Black Sea Is Where Russia's Aggression Against Ukraine Began," remarks to the NATO Parliamentary Assembly, July 4, 2017.

Visan, George, "Romania Undertakes Naval Modernization Program (Part Two)," *Eurasia Daily Monitor*, Vol. 16, No. 5, January 21, 2019. As of July 22, 2019: https://jamestown.org/program/romania-undertakes-naval-modernization-program -part-two/

Wezeman, Siemon T., and Alexandra Kuimova, *Turkey and Black Sea Security*, SIPRI Background Paper, Solna, Sweden: Stockholm International Peace Research Institute, December 2018. As of July 17, 2019: https://www.sipri.org/sites/default/files/2018-12/bp_1812_black_sea_turkey_0.pdf

Woody, Christopher, "'Good Luck, Guys': 17 Russian Jets Buzzed a British Destroyer and Left a Threatening Message Earlier This Year," *Business Insider*, November 27, 2018. As of July 15, 2019: https://www.businessinsider.com/17-russian-jets-buzzed-a-british-destroyer-in-the -black-sea-2018-11